E X P L O R I N G

ANCIENT
CIVILIZATIONS

2

Ashoka – Chang'an

Marshall Cavendish

Marshall Cavendish
99 White Plains Road
Tarrytown, New York 10591-9001

www.marshallcavendish.com

Consultants: Daud Ali, School of Oriental and African
Studies, University of London; Michael Brett, School
of Oriental and African Studies, London; John
Chinnery, School of Oriental and African Studies,
London; Philip de Souza; Joann Fletcher; Anthony
Green; Peter Groff, Department of Philosophy,
Bucknell University; Mark Handley, History
Department, University College London; Anders
Karlsson, School of Oriental and African Studies,
London; Alan Leslie, Glasgow University Archaeology
Research Department; Michael E. Smith, Department
of Anthropology, University at Albany; Matthew
Spriggs, Head of School of Archaeology and
Anthropology, Australian National University

Contributing authors: Richard Balkwill, Richard
Burrows, Peter Chrisp, Richard Dargie, Steve Eddy,
Clive Gifford, Jen Green, Peter Hicks, Robert Hull,
Jonathan Ingoldby, Pat Levy, Steven Maddocks, John
Malam, Saviour Pirotta, Stewart Ross, Sean Sheehan,
Jane Shuter

WHITE-THOMSON PUBLISHING
Editor: Alex Woolf
Design: Derek Lee
Cartographer: Peter Bull Design
Picture Research: Glass Onion Pictures
Indexer: Fiona Barr

MARSHALL CAVENDISH
Editor: Thomas McCarthy
Editorial Director: Paul Bernabeo
Production Manager: Michael Esposito

Library of Congress Cataloging-in-Publication Data
Exploring ancient civilizations.
    p. cm.
Includes bibliographical references and indexes.
  ISBN 0-7614-7456-0 (set : alk. paper) -- ISBN 0-7614-7457-9 (v. 1 :
alk. paper) -- ISBN 0-7614-7458-7 (v. 2 : alk. paper) -- ISBN
0-7614-7459-5 (v. 3 : alk. paper) -- ISBN 0-7614-7460-9 (v. 4 : alk.
paper) -- ISBN 0-7614-7461-7 (v. 5 : alk. paper) -- ISBN 0-7614-7462-5
(v. 6 : alk. paper) -- ISBN 0-7614-7463-3 (v. 7 : alk. paper) -- ISBN
0-7614-7464-1 (v. 8 : alk. paper) -- ISBN 0-7614-7465-X (v. 9 : alk.
paper) -- ISBN 0-7614-7466-8 (v. 10 : alk. paper) -- ISBN 0-7614-7467-6
(v. 11 : alk. paper)
  1. Civilization, Ancient--Encyclopedias.
  CB311.E97 2004
  930'.03--dc21

                                    2003041224

ISBN 0-7614-7456-0 (set)
ISBN 0-7614-7458-7 (vol. 2)

Printed and bound in China

07 06 05 04 03 5 4 3 2 1

Contents

Ashoka

Ashoka, or Asoka (c. 300–232 BCE), was the third king to rule over the Mauryan Empire of India. He was one of the most remarkable rulers in history, a man who tried to govern his empire in a new way – by kindness.

For more than two thousand years, Buddhists have preserved legends about King Ashoka. According to these stories, Ashoka was ruthless in his early life. In order to take the throne, he was said to have killed ninety-nine of his brothers. He was even supposed to have visited hell to learn new ways of torturing people. Ashoka then converted to Buddhism and went through a complete change of character, becoming a perfect ruler.

▶ Ashoka topped his columns with four lions, standing for his rule over the empire. This sculpture is now the national emblem of India.

Archaeological Evidence

Until the nineteenth century most historians thought that the legends of Ashoka had no more basis in truth than did fairy tales. Then, in 1837, a British scholar named James Prinsep managed to decipher a previously unknown script that had been found carved on stone pillars and rocks all over India and Pakistan. Prinsep discovered that the writings were edicts, or announcements, written by a king calling himself Devanampiya Piyadasi, meaning "Beloved of the Gods, He Who Looks On Kindly."

In one of these edicts, the king described how he had conquered a country called Kalinga. Instead of boasting about his military victory as any other ancient ruler would have, he apologized for the war, describing his sorrow at the suffering he had caused.

Some scholars guessed that this king was Ashoka, but the identification was only proved in 1915, when that name was found on one of the pillars. Ashoka was his birth name, while Devanampiya Piyadasi was the royal title he assumed on taking power.

Dharma

In his edicts Ashoka summed up his ideas in one word – dharma – meaning "right behavior." Dharma, he believed, had many aspects, including generosity, tolerance for other religions, respect for parents, and nonviolence to animals as well as people. Ashoka discouraged hunting and animal sacrifice and recommended a vegetarian diet. He appointed officials, called ministers of dharma, to spread his ideas within his empire and abroad. He also provided social services, including wells, resting places on roads, and medical treatment for people and animals.

Ashoka's reign lasted almost thirty-six years, from around 268 BCE until his death in 232. One aim in carving the edicts was to give guidance to the descendants he hoped would rule after him. He wanted them to continue his policies "so that as long as the sun and moon shall endure, men may follow the dharma" (Seventh Pillar Edict). Nevertheless, following Ashoka's death, his empire fell apart. Some historians believe that the empire was already crumbling while he was on the throne, for no edicts were carved in Ashoka's last ten years.

> On conquering Kalinga, the Beloved of the Gods felt remorse, for when an independent country is conquered, the slaughter, death, and forced removal of the people is extremely grievous to the Beloved of the Gods, and weighs heavily on his mind.... Even those who are fortunate to have escaped ... suffer from the misfortunes of their friends.... This inscription has been engraved so that any sons or great-grandsons I may have should not think of gaining new conquests.
>
> ASHOKA, THIRTEENTH ROCK EDICT, C. 256 BCE

SEE ALSO
• Buddha • Buddhism • Mauryan Empire

▼ The Great Stupa at Sanchi is a monument built by Ashoka to house some of the ashes of the Buddha. Ashoka's original brick stupa is inside this later building.

Ashur

Ashur, or Assur, was the ancient capital of Assyria. Archaeologists think the city was founded some time before 2400 BCE by a people speaking a Semitic language who migrated from the southwest into northern Mesopotamia. They used the name Ashur both for the city and for its guardian god. As their city-state grew in power, the name was also used to describe the kingdom and the people of Ashur. Assyria was the name later given to the region by the Greeks and the Romans.

A Center of Trade

During its early history Ashur, situated in present-day Iraq, was a trading city. Powerful merchant families controlled the trade in textiles and tin from northern Mesopotamia to Kanesh in Anatolia, a region in present-day eastern Turkey. Each year the donkey caravans left Ashur to make their way through the steep passes of the Taurus Mountains, returning with gold and silver. Ashur grew sufficiently wealthy and strong to police the trade routes between Mesopotamia and the Mediterranean world. The power of the merchant families faded only when the city fell to Amorite invaders in the nineteenth century BCE.

Ashur was built on a rocky outcrop overlooking the Tigris and Lesser Zab Rivers. The site was easy to defend, and the city controlled the traffic of ships on the rivers. However, good farming land in the surrounding area was limited. Water was also a problem, for the Tigris was brackish at this point and unsuitable for drinking. Later rulers moved the capital to more fertile sites. Ashur ceased to be the capital of Assyria around 863 BCE, when King Ashurnasirpal II moved his government to Calah in present-day northern Iraq.

▶ *There are five main temple sites at Ashur, as well as two vast palaces that were used by the Assyrian kings. The highest feature on the Ashur skyline was the great ziggurat, or stepped pyramid, built around 1600 BCE. Much of the site, however, has still to be excavated.*

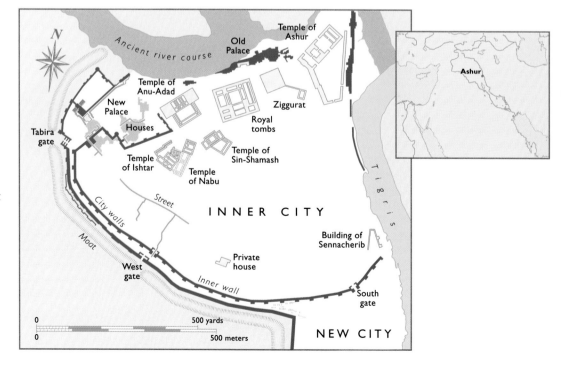

A Center of Religion

Ashur remained the religious center of the kingdom, for the city contained the shrine of the national god. The temple of the god Ashur, overlooking the Tigris River, was the most holy place in the kingdom. Prisoners of war were executed at the temple as a tribute to the god Ashur. Ashur was also an important center for the worship of the goddess Ishtar.

The Assyrian kings were buried at Ashur, and five of their tombs have been excavated on the site of the main royal palace. A surviving document from the seventh century BCE mentions that the city contained thirty-four temples and three royal palaces. Many of these buildings were rediscovered by German archaeologists between 1903 and 1914, close to the modern village of Qal'at Sherqat.

Decline

The city was eventually sacked by the Medes under Cyaxares in 614 BCE. Although it was partly inhabited again in the Parthian period, the city never prospered and was slowly lost to the sands.

TIGLATH-PILESER I
REIGNED C. 1114–C. 1076 BCE

Tiglath-pileser I was the first of the great warrior kings of Assyria. During his long reign, the border of the Assyrian kingdom was pushed as far west as Syria and the Mediterranean coast. According to legend, the king even hunted and slew a giant narwhal near the city of Byblos in Phoenicia. Like many Assyrian kings, Tiglath-pileser went on major hunting expeditions in his chariot to show his skill and bravery. On one hunt, his scribes recorded that he killed over 920 lions and 10 elephants. Tiglath-pileser, like many later kings of Assyria, was known for his cruelty. Many of the peoples he had conquered rose up in rebellion after his death.

SEE ALSO
- Assyrians • Calah • Ishtar
- Parthians

◄ *In this relief, Ashurnasirpal II stands beneath the winged disk that may have represented the god Ashur. In his hands he holds two symbols of his kingship, the royal scepter and his hunting bow. Assyrian kings wore a conical cap with a small horned top when performing religious ceremonies and public rituals.*

Ashurbanipal

Ashurbanipal (reigned 668–c. 627 BCE) was the last great king of Assyria. He came to the Assyrian throne upon the death of his father, Esarhaddon. To keep the peace, his brother Shamash-shum-ukin was given the throne of Babylon, which was under Assyrian control at that time. However, Ashurbanipal was in full command of the mighty Assyrian army, and so he held the real power in the land.

Wars of Conquest

With Ashurbanipal at its head, the Assyrian army ruthlessly sacked Thebes, the capital of Egypt, in 665 BCE. The Egyptians never recovered from the devastation. Ashurbanipal's men carried off a fabulous amount of treasure. Much of it was used to decorate the Assyrian capital of Nineveh.

Jealous of his brother's success, Shamash-shum-ukin, ruler of Babylon, plotted against Ashurbanipal in 652 BCE. This rivalry led to four bitter years of civil war before Babylon fell. Shamash-shum-ukin burned to death in his own palace.

Ashurbanipal's men marched on to yet another war. This time the enemy was the Elamites to the east. In 639 BCE, after nine years of war, the Elamite king was beheaded, and his royal city of Susa was razed to the ground. Ashurbanipal planned to destroy Elam forever. The statues of its gods were carried off to Nineveh, and the graves of its kings were opened and ruined. Ashurbanipal even boasted that he had spread salt and a prickly plant called *sikhlu* over the fields of Elam so that nothing could ever grow there again.

◀ *Ashurbanipal riding in his chariot in a seventh-century BCE relief discovered at Nineveh. Assyrian kings were often shown in their chariots. Chariots with light, spoked wheels were invented in the early second millennium BCE. They were well suited to the hard, dry roads of Assyria and Babylonia.*

The Scholarly King

Although he was a successful warrior, Ashurbanipal was also a scholar. He enjoyed solving mathematical problems, and he learned to read the Akkadian and ancient Sumerian languages. He sent out agents to collect cuneiform tablets from the schools and temples around his kingdom. Copies of these writings were sent back to his library at Nineveh. Thanks to Ashurbanipal, thousands of Mesopotamian texts have survived, including the ancient Babylonian *Creation Epic* and *Gilgamesh Epic*.

The arts also flourished under Ashurbanipal. Like other Assyrian kings, he was shown in royal sculptures as a brave warrior and hunter. However, Ashurbanipal also appears as a family man at rest with his wife in his beloved garden at Nineveh. Only the severed head of an enemy king hanging from a nearby tree reminds us of the fear inspired by this monarch.

Legacy

Ashurbanipal's reign was the highest point in Assyria's history. By 635 BCE Nineveh was the capital of a vast empire that stretched from Anatolia in the north to the Persian Gulf and upper Egypt in the south. Its old rivals had all been destroyed. However, the Assyrian kingdom was exhausted after thirty years of war. It was further weakened by twelve years of rebellion after the great king died or left the throne around 627 BCE.

SEE ALSO

▲ *Many of the sculptures in Ashurbanipal's palace at Nineveh commemorate his campaigns in Egypt in the 660s and 650s BCE. Assyrian troops use siege ladders to scale the walls of an Egyptian city while enemies tumble from the ramparts to their death. Egyptian prisoners are led away into slavery.*

IN LATER LIFE ASHURBANIPAL DESCRIBED THE TRAINING FOR KINGSHIP HE HAD RECEIVED IN HIS YOUTH:

... I studied the heavens with the learned masters ... I solved the laborious problems of division and multiplication ... I read the script of Sumer and the difficult Akkadian, taking pleasure in reading the stones from before the Flood ... I held the bow ... I let fly the arrow ... I hurled heavy lances like a javelin. Holding the reins like a driver, I made the chariot wheels go round. ... At the same time, I was learning how to behave like a king.

FROM AN ANCIENT ASSYRIAN INSCRIPTION

Assyrians

The first Assyrians were a nomadic people who settled along the Tigris River in northern Mesopotamia around 2500 BCE. By 1850 BCE this region was very prosperous because of its key position on the trade routes between the Persian Gulf and the Mediterranean Sea. Assyrian merchants in Ashur and other city-states grew rich on the profits of the tin and copper trade. Their caravans carried these valuable metals to distant cities in Anatolia, Phoenicia, and Egypt.

Early Assyria was swept away after 1750 BCE by attacks from Babylonian and Mitanni invaders. After enduring several centuries of foreign rule, Assyria became independent again around 1350 BCE. Assyrian kings learned to use fear and terror to help hold back their foes. They boasted of their severe cruelty to rebels, who were beheaded, impaled on stakes, or thrust into the city ovens alive. Thousands of prisoners of war were slaughtered in tribute to the Assyrian supreme god, Ashur. Whole peoples were uprooted from their cities and deported or marched at sword point to other parts of the kingdom. By 900 BCE the Assyrians were the most feared people in the region.

Period of Domination

The great age of Assyria began in 911 BCE, when Adad-nirari II defeated Babylon and the other smaller kingdoms of Mesopotamia, such as that of the Aramaeans. For most of the next three hundred years, Assyria was the strongest military power in western Asia.

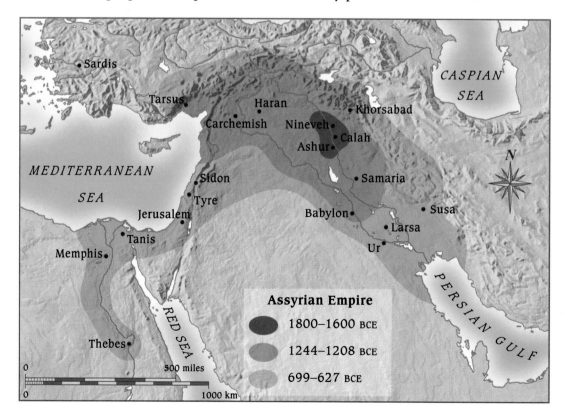

▶ A map of the Assyrian kingdom showing the three periods of Assyrian power.

Sardis
Tarsus
Haran
Khorsabad
CASPIAN SEA
Carchemish
Nineveh
Calah
Ashur
MEDITERRANEAN SEA
Sidon
Tyre
Samaria
Jerusalem
Babylon
Susa
Larsa
Tanis
Ur
Memphis
RED SEA
PERSIAN GULF
Thebes

Assyrian Empire
1800–1600 BCE
1244–1208 BCE
699–627 BCE

0   500 miles
0   1000 km

3500 3000 2500 2000 1500 1000 500 1 500

ASSYRIA

c. 2400 BCE

City of Ashur founded on the western bank of the upper Tigris.

c. 1800 BCE

Shamshi-Adad I makes Assyria into the strongest power in northern Mesopotamia.

c. 1750–1500 BCE

Assyria falls under control of Babylonian and Mitanni invaders.

c. 1350 BCE

Ashur-uballit I and Shalmaneser I restore Assyrian independence.

1114–1076 BCE

Tiglath-pileser I rebuilds a vast Assyrian kingdom across western Asia.

c. 725 BCE

Assyrians capture Israel and deport the Israelite nation to Mesopotamia.

710 BCE

Sargon II moves the Assyrian capital to the newly built city of Dur Sharrukin.

689 BCE

Sennacherib sacks Babylon and carries its riches off to Nineveh.

665 BCE

Assyrians capture and destroy Thebes, the capital of ancient Egypt.

639 BCE

The Assyrian kingdom reaches its greatest extent with the capture of Susa.

612 BCE

The Assyrian army defeated by a joint attack of the Medes and Babylonians.

612 BCE

Fall of the city of Nineveh. The Assyrian court moved to Harran.

c. 610 BCE

Fall of the city of Harran. Final collapse of Assyria.

ASHUR

The first Assyrians were desert nomads who worshiped Ashur as their god. When they built their first large settlement, Ashur became the god of the city that took his name. Assyrians believed that Ashur had the power to defeat the legions of demons and evil spirits that tormented the human world. The god's great temple of Ekur in the citadel at Ashur was the holiest place in Assyria. However, Ashur was a cruel god and many prisoners of war were tortured, mutilated, and executed at Ekur to calm his anger. The kings of Assyria were also the high priests of Ashur. Many kings, such as Ashurbanipal, used the name of the god in their own royal name.

◀ An eighth-century BCE winged bull with human head from the palace of Sargon II at Khorsabad, now in the Louvre, Paris. These colossal stone statues weighed as much as sixteen tons. They usually had five legs so that they could be viewed both from the front, as standing still, and from the side, as walking forwards.

Warrior kings such as Ashurnasirpal II and Sargon II built vast new cities at Calah and Dur Sharrukin (near modern Khorsabad) with the stream of riches and plunder that poured into Assyria. The Assyrian city of Nineveh was probably the largest city in the world in the seventh century BCE.

Art and Sculpture

The Assyrians were not simply fearsome warriors. The library at Nineveh brought together, and preserved, much of the learning of the ancient world. Assyrian artists were talented sculptors who decorated the walls of their public buildings with a great number of magnificent sculptures and carvings. Assyrian sculpture reached a high point between the ninth and seventh centuries, when bas-reliefs (shallow relief carvings) lined the walls of the royal palaces at cities such as Calah and Nineveh.

Beliefs

The Assyrians were a very superstitious people who believed that evil spirits, or demons, moved in the human world spreading bad luck and disease. If a demon took over someone's body, then the family of the affected person had to send for the *ashipu* or *mushmushu*. These special priests knew how to produce the mixture of blood, dirt, rotten meat, and excrement that was used as a potion to chase away the demon.

Later Assyrians thought that these spirits were ghosts of people who had not been buried properly or who had died in an unhappy way, such as hanging. To prevent these ghosts from coming into their home, Assyrian families took great care to bury their dead properly. The corpse was sometimes sealed into a large pottery coffin with gifts of wine and tasty sweetmeats. The coffin was then carefully buried under the floor of the family dwelling.

The king was just as superstitious as the poorest peasant. He had to observe four taboo days in every month when the laws of religion decided what he could eat, wear, and do. If the king broke the taboo, his kingdom might be cursed.

◀ *This bronze statuette is inscribed "I am Pazuzu, son of Hanbi, king of the evil wind demons." Despite these words, Pazuzu could be turned to good purposes. Assyrian women wore amulets of Pazuzu to protect them in childbirth.*

Food and Farming

Most Assyrian peasants were farmers who grew their own food to survive. Assyria received just enough rainfall each summer to ensure good crops. The Assyrians built dams and reservoirs to conserve their water for as long as possible. Getting drinking water to the cities was a problem, for the slow Tigris waters were marshy in many places and not good to drink. The Assyrians built long aqueducts to convey fresher water from the hill streams to Nineveh.

SENNACHERIB, KING OF ASSYRIA, DESCRIBES HOW HIS ARMY DESTROYED BABYLON IN 689 BCE:

Like a hurricane, I attacked the city, and like a storm, I destroyed it ... I did not spare its inhabitants, young and old, and I filled the streets of the city with their corpses ... I devastated the town itself and its houses from their foundations to their roofs ... I destroyed and overthrew everything by fire. ... In order that in future even the soil of its temples be forgotten, I ravaged it with water and turned it into pastures.

FROM AN ASSYRIAN MEMORIAL CELEBRATING SENNACHERIB'S VICTORY.

◀ Archers were very important troops in the Assyrian army. They had to be able to use their bows on horseback and from chariots. Assyrian youths were sent to hunt birds and animals in the forest, as hunting was a useful way of acquiring skill with the bow.

THE ASSYRIAN ARMY

Unlike some other ancient peoples, the Assyrians had a professional army. The soldiers were well organized and well equipped. As they were paid to do a full-time job of soldiering, after a battle they did not need to go back to their farms to make their living. Instead they trained for their next campaign.

By the seventh century BCE the Assyrian king could call on an experienced force of almost 400,000 men in times of war. His force was made up of lightly armed archers and slingers, heavily mailed lancers, daggermen, cavalry, and charioteers. There were fortresses in each of the main Assyrian cities containing vast stores of weapons and supplies for these troops.

A unit of army engineers laid out unobstructed roads across the kingdom and built an awesome range of siege machines. The engineers also kept the Assyrian fleet of war chariots ready to carry their teams of driver, bowman, and spearman into action. The army even made and stored boats made of tarred reeds and inflatable goatskins so that the troops could cross the rivers of Mesopotamia in the flood season.

Fast army couriers carried orders and news by horse, while fire beacons were used to carry signals in wartime. Assyria had enemies on all its borders, and the army spent most summers on campaign. It is no wonder that one writer has called war "the national industry of Assyria."

▶ A kilted Assyrian warrior armed with bow and dagger with his legs protected by bronze greaves. Lightly armed troops of this kind were an important part of the army of Sargon II that conquered much of western Asia in the eighth century BCE.

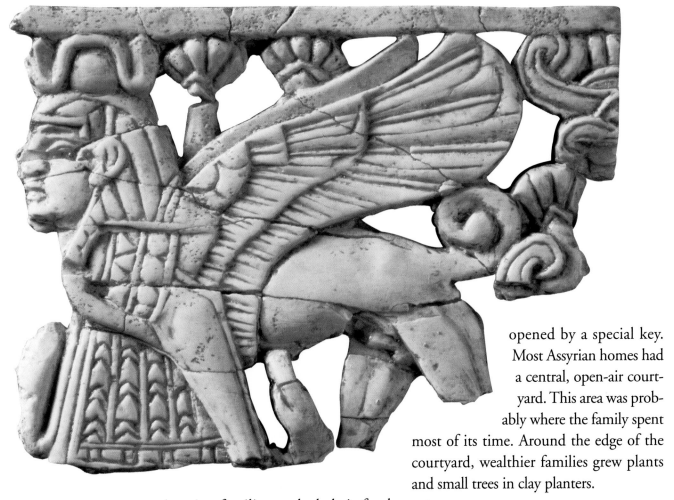

▲ Thousands of ivory carvings have been excavated at the Assyrian city of Calah, representing the work of artists from many areas of the empire. Ancient artists liked carving ivory because it was strong but flexible. Small pieces of ivory could be carved in detail, then joined together to form a larger sculpture.

opened by a special key. Most Assyrian homes had a central, open-air courtyard. This area was probably where the family spent most of its time. Around the edge of the courtyard, wealthier families grew plants and small trees in clay planters.

Assyrian families cooked their food over an open fire in small clay pots. Strips of unleavened barley dough were laid over a hot clay pot to bake. Most meals consisted of fruits, including dates and figs, cheese, and a mixture of vegetables, such as onions, olives, cucumber, and lentils. Meat, including pork, mutton, beef, goose, pigeon, and duck, was butchered regularly. Archaeologists believe that the Assyrians invented the process of distillation and used it to make a kind of brandy from local fruits. They also brewed beer and drank large amounts of goat's milk.

Houses and Homes

Most Assyrians lived in one-story houses made of mud bricks. Around the eighth century BCE the Assyrians discovered how to make primitive locks that could only be

Decline

Assyria enjoyed its greatest power and wealth in the seventh century BCE under King Ashurbanipal. However, his great kingdom was almost entirely swept away in a joint attack by the Medes and the Babylonians only fifteen years after the end of his reign around 627 BCE. By 612 Ashur, Nineveh, and probably Calah, had been sacked. Although Assyria had been beaten many times in its long history, it failed to recover from this devastating defeat. It never recovered its independence.

SEE ALSO

- Aqueducts • Ashur • Ashurbanipal • Calah
- Mesopotamia • Nineveh
- Sargon of Akkad • Sennacherib

Astronomy

Astronomy, the study of planets and stars and their movement in the skies, is the oldest of the physical sciences. The early Chinese, Egyptians, Babylonians, and – later – the Greeks, all had accurate ways of observing the skies.

Ancient peoples believed that the sun and the stars were gods who controlled the destiny of human beings. Astronomers, who were usually priests, made great attempts to understand and foretell their movements around the sky. For thousands of years, astronomy and astrology – the art of predicting the future through the stars – were treated as the same subject.

By 3000 BCE the Babylonians could accurately predict lunar eclipses, which they interpreted as signs of impending doom. In 2296 BCE the Chinese recorded the first sighting of a comet, and this phenomenon was seen as proof that the gods in the skies were angry. Between 1600 and 1551 BCE astrologers in Mesopotamia identified a belt of twelve constellations, which they named the zodiac. The astrologers used it to tell people's future, and it remains the basis on which horoscopes are cast to this day.

Shape and Position of the Earth

Early astronomers believed that the world was a flat disk surrounded by a ring of ocean. Below the world was a vast abyss; above it were the heavens with all their stars. The ancient Greeks challenged this belief. They were the first true astronomers, interested in finding out how the universe worked, not in predicting the future.

Between 520 and 511 BCE, a Greek astronomer named Anaximander insisted that the earth was not a flat disk but was shaped like a slightly bent cylinder. A few years later the philosopher Pythagoras and his followers were teaching that the world was a sphere. Aristotle, an influential philosopher born in Macedonia in 384 BCE, supported this view. So did Ptolemy, another Greek astronomer, who was born in 85 CE.

◀ *A Babylonian globe from around 500 BCE shows the flat world ringed by the ocean, the home of the early gods. The circles around the rim represent mountains. Now housed in the British Museum, the globe was originally part of a public building.*

Ptolemy used the works of previous astronomers to write a book called *The Almagest*. In this book he proposed a theory now known as the Ptolemaic system. His theory placed the earth at the center of the universe. The sun and the five planets in the solar system that had been discovered by then revolved around it. Beyond them, the stars were fixed to a big celestial sphere. The Ptolemaic system remained undisputed until it was challenged by the Polish astronomer Copernicus in the sixteenth century CE.

SEE ALSO

• Aristotle • Ptolemy • Pythagoras • Science

ARISTARCHUS OF SAMOS
C. 310–C. 230 BCE

Long before Copernicus there was one astronomer and mathematician who did not believe that the planets moved around the earth. His name was Aristarchus of Samos. Around 280 BCE he suggested that the earth rotated around the sun. The theory did not find favor with astronomers of the time.

Aristarchus was born on the island of Samos in Greece around 310 BCE. He was a follower of Pythagoras, and he sought to understand the universe through geometry and arithmetic. The only book by Aristarchus still in existence is *On the Dimensions and Distances of the Moon and the Sun*, which describes a way of measuring the distances of the moon and the sun from the earth. Although Aristarchus's calculations were wrong, his theory of using angles for measurement was accurate.

Athena

Athena was the goddess of war and wisdom in ancient Greek mythology. The Greeks also called her Pallas Athene, and the Romans called her Minerva. We know about Athena from ancient Greek writings, especially Homer's long poems, the *Iliad* and the *Odyssey*.

Athena was also the goddess of handicrafts such as weaving and metalwork. Her symbol was the owl, because of her wisdom. She was one of the most powerful Greek gods and the favorite of Zeus, the king of the gods, who was her father. Athena was higher ranked than Ares, another war god, who lacked Athena's wisdom, and she often got the better of the sea god, Poseidon.

According to myth, the Greek city of Athens was named after Athena when she beat Poseidon in a contest. He demonstrated his power by creating a well of saltwater. Athena showed hers by planting an olive tree, which was judged to be more useful.

Athena's Birth

Athena's mother was Metis, the goddess of intelligence. Zeus learned that Metis was to have a child by him, and fearing the fulfillment of a prophecy that he would lose his throne to a son of hers, he swallowed Metis whole. Zeus eventually gave birth to Athena from his head, which had to be split open. The infant Athena leaped out fully armed, giving her battle cry.

Help and Inspiration

Athena helped human beings by advising or inspiring them in battle. She gave the hero Perseus a polished shield to use as a mirror so that he could kill a monster called Medusa without looking directly at her terrible face. Athena later carried Medusa's head on her own shield as a trophy. She also inspired Diomedes to victory in the Trojan War and helped Odysseus return home after the same war.

▶ *In this marble statue, Athena's left hand points to the heavens, the source of her wisdom. Her right hand offers wisdom to humankind.*

Punisher of Mortals

Athena sometimes punished mortals, although she often took pity on them afterwards. She blinded Teiresias for seeing her naked but then granted him wisdom and the power to see the future. On another occasion, when a woman named Arachne challenged Athena to a weaving contest, Athena made her so ashamed that she hanged herself. Afterwards Athena brought Arachne back to life as a spider.

How Athena Was Worshiped

Athena was worshiped throughout Greece but especially in Athens, where three temples were dedicated to her: the Parthenon, the Erechtheion, and the Temple of Nike. In one of her festivals, two girls carried a basket of mysterious objects to an underground chamber. In another ceremony priests and priestesses walked beneath a huge parasol. A third featured a procession of priests, magistrates, girls, and young men. They offered gifts to Athena, and there were games, music, and dancing.

IN THIS PASSAGE FROM THE *ILIAD*, HOMER DESCRIBES HOW ATHENA HELPED GREEK WARRIORS IN THE TROJAN WAR:

Then Pallas Athena put courage into the heart of Diomedes, son of Tydeus, so that he would outshine all the other Greeks and cover himself with glory. She made a stream of fire flare from his shield and helmet like the star that shines most brilliantly in summer after its bath in the great ocean. She kindled a similar fire on his head and shoulders as she urged him speed into the thickest hurly-burly of the battle.

ILIAD, BOOK 5

SEE ALSO
- Athens
- Iliad and Odyssey
- Mythology
- Odysseus
- Zeus

◀ *The Temple of Athena Nike is the smallest of three temples on the Acropolis in Athens. Athena was worshiped here in her role as bringer of victory. Nike (Victory) was sometimes regarded as a separate goddess; at other times she merged with Athena.*

Athens

Athens is the capital of modern Greece. In ancient times it was a powerful city-state, part of Attica, and the center of ancient Greek civilization. Little is known about Athens before the ninth century BCE. Like other Greek states, it was originally ruled by kings. However, between the eleventh and ninth centuries BCE, the monarchy was overthrown. Gradually reforms were introduced, and power came to be shared among a wider number of people.

Democracy

In the sixth century BCE, largely through the work of the statesmen Solon and Cleisthenes, Athens became a democracy – a state in which ordinary citizens held power (although women and slaves were excluded). A council of five hundred citizens was chosen annually, but their proposals had to be voted upon by a people's assembly at a place called the Pnyx, where any citizen could speak. Cleisthenes introduced a method for getting rid of unpopular citizens. Citizens could be banished from Athens for up to ten years if their name was scratched, by a majority of people, on ostraca, which were broken pieces of pottery. From this we get the word *ostracism*.

The Delian League

At Marathon in 490 BCE, the small Athenian army successfully defended themselves and all of Greece against an invasion by the Persians, but when the Persians returned in 480 BCE, the Athenians had to abandon their city, and it was destroyed. However, the Athenian navy, helped by some other Greek states, then lured the Persian fleet into the narrow waters of Salamis and overwhelmed it.

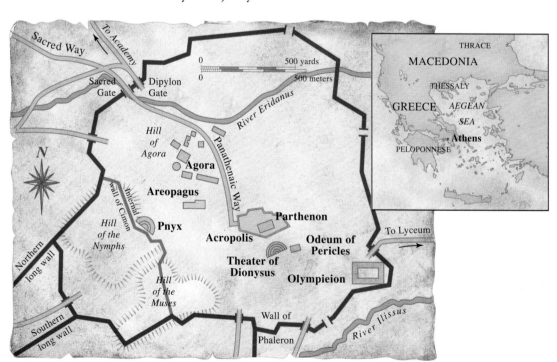

▶ City plan of ancient Athens.

◀ The Theater of
Dionysus in Athens. At the
top of the steps, there
would have been a long
narrow stage, with a
stage building, the skene,
behind. In the large
semicircular area the
fifteen men of the chorus
would sing, dance, and
comment on the stage
action.

After this victory the Athenians organized an alliance with the other Greek states – the Delian League – to protect Greece against any future Persian threat. Each state contributed ships or money toward the building of a new fleet. When the Persian threat had passed, Athens insisted on continuing to collect the tribute from the other states, in return for Athenian protection. The Athenians used much of this money to rebuild the holy buildings on the rocky outcrop at the center of their city, known as the Acropolis. These buildings included a magnificent temple dedicated to Athena, called the Parthenon, built between 447 and 432 BCE, with a wonderfully sculpted image of the goddess inside.

A Center of Arts and Learning

Cultural life flourished in Athens during the fifth century BCE. Drama competitions in the open-air theater on the slopes of the Acropolis attracted playwrights such as Sophocles, Euripides, and Aristophanes. In the gymnasia Athenians looked after their bodies as well as their minds, for here many of Athens's great philosophers, such as Socrates, would discuss matters with any

who wanted to listen. Athletics was very important to the Athenians, as it was to many Greeks, and every four years games were held in honor of Athena, with competitions similar to the Olympics. Below the Acropolis was the agora, a shopping and government center.

LAW COURTS

Athenian democracy extended to the law courts. Jurors were randomly selected by a special machine in the morning and sent to one of the courts. There were at least 201 jurymen for each court because it was believed that such a large number would be difficult to threaten or bribe. There were no judges or lawyers, only a chairman. The jurors would first listen to arguments from both sides, with speeches timed by a simple water clock. After the arguments, with no discussion, the jurors would vote "guilty" or "not guilty" by handing in a token.

POTTERY

Athenian pottery was famous. Black-figure work had the outline of a picture first painted with slip, a watered-down mixture of clay and ash, and then the details were scratched through. In the firing process the slip baked black while the rest of the pot turned red, including the scratched detail. In red-figure painting, the detail of the picture was painted on, and then the rest of the pot was covered with slip, which would later turn black. Black-figure pictures often look simple, like silhouettes; red figure has more flowing lines.

▶ This pot depicts the birth of the goddess Athena, who sprang fully grown from Zeus's head. The pot is black-figure work with other colors added. The natural red of the clay is seen behind the figures, while the rest of the pot has been painted black.

War with Sparta

By the middle of the fifth century BCE, Athens and its rival city-state, Sparta, were at war. The Athenians built fortified walls, known as the Long Walls, from the city to the harbor, a distance of nearly five miles. When the Spartans invaded, the Athenians confidently retreated behind the walls. However, there was an outbreak of plague in which thousands of Athenians lost their lives, including their greatest statesman, Pericles.

In 415 BCE Athens invaded Syracuse, a Greek colony in Sicily and an ally of Sparta. The invasion was a disaster. The Athenians lost 20,000 troops and more than two hundred ships. In 404 BCE, Athens was finally defeated. However, the Spartans did not destroy the city or kill or enslave its citizens, for they remembered the heroic role the Athenians had played at Marathon and Salamis.

During the fourth century BCE Athens continued to prosper, although the city was no longer a great power. Plato, a disciple of Socrates, was a famous philosopher of that time. During the Roman period the city continued to be recognized as one of the finest centers of learning in the world.

SEE ALSO

- Acropolis • Athena • Cities • Drama
- Greece, Classical • Greek Philosophy
- Olympia • Pericles • Plato • Socrates
- Sparta • Sports and Entertainment

Attila

Attila the Hun (406–453 CE) was one of the fiercest warriors the world has ever known. As king of the Huns, he nearly brought the whole Roman Empire crashing to its knees. It was said that no one, barbarian or Roman, could look him in the eye without flinching.

Early Conquests

During the time of Attila, the Huns controlled a large part of western Asia, from the Alps in the west to the Caspian Sea in the east. Attila's uncle, Rugila, died in 434 CE, and Attila and his brother Bleda became joint kings.

The Huns were being paid by the Roman emperor to protect the frontier of the eastern Roman Empire on the river Danube. Attila's first act was to demand double the money. In 441 the Romans made the mistake of not paying, and Attila marched over the border. Over the next two years he inflicted a lot of damage on the Romans and destroyed several of their cities. The emperor Theodosius II agreed to pay Attila all of the money owed and a lot more besides.

It is not known how or why, but in 445 Attila murdered Bleda. In 447, as sole king, Attila set off on another rampage. The Huns ripped down monasteries and churches and slaughtered monks and nuns. By 449 they had devastated large areas of the eastern Roman Empire.

The Invasion of Gaul

In 451 Attila decided to invade Gaul (present-day France and Belgium). At that time, Gaul was split between the Romans and the Visigoths. Expecting the worst, the Roman general Aetius made a pact with the Visigothic king. Meanwhile, Attila united his Huns with other tribes he had subdued. His barbarian force marched west, destroying city after city.

▼ Attila was said to be bad-tempered, aggressive, and obstinate. The Romans called him Scourge of God.

The two massive armies met outside the city of Chalôns in southern France in 451. The Battle of Chalôns was one of the most horrific battles of ancient times. Some historians estimate that 300,000 soldiers were killed. Thanks to Aetius's outstanding military tactics, Attila suffered his first major defeat.

The Italian Invasion

The following year, Attila was as ambitious and aggressive as ever. He marched south on another trail of destruction. His sights were set on Rome, the greatest prize of all. In a bid to save his city, Pope Leo I marched north over the hills into the Huns' camp. He ordered Attila to turn back, and Attila did. Some stories say that Attila saw a vision of St Peter above the Pope's head, and the fearless warrior was actually frightened. Others deny this account and say that Attila withdrew

THIS DESCRIPTION OF ATTILA IS BASED ON AN ANCIENT ACCOUNT:

... a large head, a swarthy complexion, small, deep-seated eyes, a flat nose, a few hairs in the place of a beard, broad shoulders, and a short square body. ... He had a custom of fiercely rolling his eyes, as if he wished to enjoy the terror which he inspired. ... He delighted in war.

because he was worried about the famine and disease raging in Italy at the time. Either way, Europe was once again saved from the Huns. In 453 Attila died in his sleep. Those who buried him were killed so that nobody would find his body.

▲ One of the great heroes of the Battle of Chalôns was young Thorismund, a Visigoth prince. This picture, painted in the nineteenth century, shows a scene after the battle, when the Visigoths raised Thorismund up on their shields and proclaimed him king.

SEE ALSO
• Huns

Augustine of Hippo

In the first few hundred years after the death of Jesus Christ, the struggle to establish Christianity in the Roman Empire was led by certain bishops and teachers, known as the church fathers. One of the greatest of these was Augustine of Hippo (354–430 CE). Augustine converted to Christianity at the age of thirty-three.

For almost half his life, Augustine was bishop of the city of Hippo, which is now in Algeria. As he delivered impassioned sermons in his small North African church, defending his ideas against his opponents, he could not have foreseen that one day those ideas would become a foundation of the Christian Church.

His Life

Augustine was born in Tagaste in eastern Numidia (modern Tunisia). He went to Carthage to study. His favorite subject was rhetoric, and his favorite writer was Cicero, a brilliant Roman writer and politician. Augustine became a great scholar, and when he was thirty, he was appointed professor of rhetoric at the emperor's court in Milan. There he met Ambrose, another church father, and together they read the Bible. Two years after arriving in Milan, Augustine fell ill and went to recover in a country villa nearby. He spent his time thinking about Christianity, and the following year, on Easter Saturday 387, he was baptized.

▼ This sixteenth-century Italian painting shows Saint Augustine writing a letter. Augustine is interrupted by the voice of Saint Jerome, telling him that he will soon die and go to heaven.

An illustration for an eleventh-century manuscript of City of God. Christ is on the throne at the top of the illustration. The manuscript is held in the Medicea-Laurenziana Library in Florence, Italy.

In 389 the people of Hippo Regius begged Augustine to be their priest. He accepted, and in 395 he was made bishop. His main job was to teach his congregation. However, as bishop he also had an important position within the Christian Church as a whole.

For the next thirty-four years, until he died, Augustine fought for his belief that the Church should be "catholic," which means "embracing all." His writings were distributed everywhere in the Roman Empire and helped ensure the inclusion of his views as a major part of the doctrine of Christianity to this day.

Works of Augustine

A classical education left Augustine highly skilled in philosophy and rhetoric. He was the first great classical writer to apply these skills to Christian subjects. Thousands of his sermons, drawing lessons from the Bible, still exist. One of his most famous works is *Confessions* (397), in which he tells the story of his youth and his conversion to Christianity. It shows that he was influenced by the Greek philosopher Plato.

Between 413 and 427 he wrote his masterpiece, *City of God*, which states that though all human-built cities must eventually crumble and fall, the city of God is eternal. As Augustine lay dying in 430, his own city of Hippo was being attacked. The sun was setting on the Roman Empire, but rising on the church he helped create.

SEE ALSO

- Christianity • Cicero • Constantine
- Jesus of Nazareth • Plato
- Roman Philosophy
- Roman Republic and Empire • Religion

Augustus

Augustus (63 BCE–14 CE) was the first emperor of ancient Rome. He came to power in 27 BCE and ruled the empire for nearly forty-one years. His reign brought peace and prosperity to Rome but also marked the end of the Roman Republic.

Early Life and Rise to Power

Augustus's original name was Gaius Octavius, and concerning his early life historians usually refer to him as Octavian. His mother was Julius Caesar's niece. Julius Caesar thought highly of Octavian, and he planned to give Octavian a senior command in his army. However, before he could do so, Caesar was assassinated. Caesar's will revealed that he had adopted Octavian as his son, greatly increasing the young man's importance as a potential successor.

Driven by ambition and a desire for revenge, Octavian – who was only nineteen at the time of Caesar's death – embarked on a course of action that was to see him become the most powerful man in the world. In Rome he found power in the hands of two generals, Mark Antony and Aemilius Lepidus. Rather than attempt to defeat them in battle, Octavian formed a pact with them. Their combined armies then defeated Caesar's assassins, Brutus and Cassius, at the Battle of Philippi in northern Greece in 42 BCE.

IN HIS BIOGRAPHY OF AUGUSTUS, *THE LIFE OF THE DEIFIED AUGUSTUS*, SUETONIUS DESCRIBES THE EMPEROR:

He was unusually handsome and exceedingly graceful at all periods of his life, though he cared nothing for personal adornment. He was so far from being particular about the dressing of his hair that he would have several barbers working in a hurry at the same time ... while ... he would either be reading or writing something.

▼ One of the most famous images of Augustus is this marble statue from Livia's villa at Prima Porta, near Rome. It is now on display in the Vatican Gallery in Rome.

A cameo of Augustus's wife, Livia. Despite her loyalty to her husband, Livia was suspected of arranging the deaths of Augustus's son-in-law Marcellus and his grandsons Gaius and Lucius so that her own son, Tiberius, could become Augustus's heir after the death of Agrippa.

The three victors divided the empire between them. Not long after this battle, Lepidus was stripped of his military power for trying to defy Octavian, and the Roman world belonged to Octavian and Antony.

The Battle of Actium

Despite his marriage to Octavian's sister, Antony fell in love with Queen Cleopatra of Egypt, and he remained there, living a life of luxury and excess. Such behavior was regarded as very un-Roman. When Octavian denounced Antony as a traitor in the Roman senate, the senate agreed to declare war on Cleopatra.

Octavian's forces met Antony's at Actium on the west coast of Greece on September 2, 31 BCE. Octavian won, and the following year Antony and Cleopatra both committed suicide in Egypt. Octavian was now effectively sole ruler of the empire.

Stability and the "Golden Age"

The fate of Julius Caesar taught Octavian that if he set himself up as a dictator and ignored the wishes of the senate, he would not last very long. So he publicly gave up his power to the senate, which then promptly returned it to him. The senators knew that Octavian held the real power, as he commanded the armies and controlled the provinces, and without him there would be more civil wars. Octavian's approach was clever: it allowed the senate to retain its pride and made him appear to be in favor of democracy.

In 27 BCE Octavian was given the title Augustus, meaning "sacred" – a great public honor. In 19 BCE the senate persuaded him to become the head of state, and the stage was set for the Augustan Age.

Between 19 BCE and his death in 14 CE, Augustus repaired and rebuilt Rome. He improved sanitation, constructed new buildings, and streamlined the city's civil administration. As famously claimed, he "found Rome brick and left it marble." He also brought about religious and moral reforms whose aim was to revive traditional Roman values, such as hard work and faithful marriage.

Augustus lived up to these values himself: according to the historian Suetonius he lived simply in a "modest dwelling ... without any marble decorations or handsome pavements." He ate simply, drank little, and even banished his own daughter and granddaughter because they had committed adultery. His own marriage, to Livia Drusilla, lasted over fifty years, from 38 BCE to the emperor's death.

Augustus the God

When Augustus died, he was deified (declared a god). This was the greatest honor the senate and people could give. His legacy is immense. His reforms of the state and the military ensured that the empire would endure. During his reign the empire expanded, and Roman-controlled territory extended farther than ever before. Under him the arts flourished, with poets such as Virgil and Horace producing some of the greatest Latin literature ever written. His building program gave Rome some of its greatest monuments, including the Forum of Augustus with its Temple of Mars Ultor (the Avenger) and the Temple of Apollo on the Palatine.

SEE ALSO

• Aeneid • Antony, Mark • Caesar, Julius
• Cleopatra • Roman Republic and Empire

MARCUS AGRIPPA
c. 62–12 BCE

Agrippa was Augustus's lifelong friend and his chief military commander. He played a key role in the defeat of Antony at Actium. Once peace was established, Agrippa assisted Augustus in his building program and supervised many important projects. They included the construction of harbors, roads, and public buildings and making major improvements to Rome's water supply.

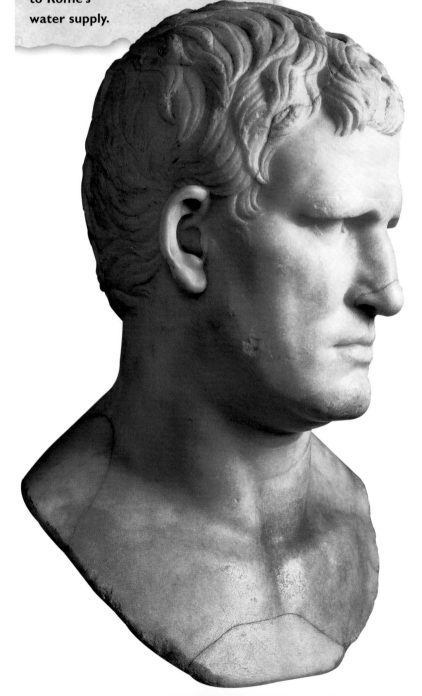

▼ A portrait bust of Agrippa. Augustus knew that if no natural heir survived him, Agrippa would assume power. To secure this agreement Agrippa (then aged forty) married Augustus's sixteen-year-old daughter, Julia.

Avebury

Few monuments in prehistoric Europe evoke more interest than stone circles, the largest of which is at Avebury in southern Britain. It was built on a vast scale some 4,800 years ago. Such is Avebury's importance that in 1986 it was designated a World Heritage Site by UNESCO.

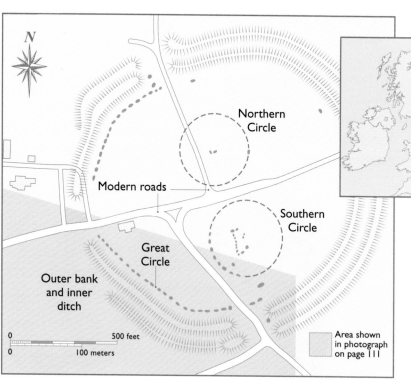

Area shown in photograph on page 111

▲ *As the map shows, modern roads have had only marginal impact on the prehistoric structures and earthworks at Avebury.*

The Setting

Avebury is in the English county of Wiltshire, twenty-four miles (38 km) north of Stonehenge, an equally famous circle of stones. While the circle at Stonehenge is small and tall, Avebury is big and wide, covering an area of 28.5 acres (11.5 hectares). It is so big that a small village sits comfortably inside the monument, which measures four-fifths of a mile (1,300 m) all around. In the immediate vicinity of Avebury, there are other monuments of Neolithic date, including an ancient tomb and an enormous earth mound, indicating that this area was a center of intense activity and importance. In Britain the Neolithic period spans the timescale from roughly 3500 to 1700 BCE.

Building Avebury

The building of Avebury was a huge undertaking, requiring great organization and physical effort. One estimate suggests it took 1.5 million person-hours to complete it. Avebury is actually several interrelated structures, built over a period of five hundred years between about 2800 and 2300 BCE. Surrounding the whole site is a massive earthwork. It consists of a high bank and a steep-sided ditch, dug into the chalk bedrock with antler picks and shovels made from the shoulder blades of cattle. The ditch was originally thirty feet (9 m) deep.

Visitors entered the site through four pathways in the bank and ditch. Within the enclosure are three circles of standing stones. The largest, or Great Circle, measuring 1,300 feet (400 m) across, contains ninety-eight megaliths of unshaped sarsen rock, the heaviest of which weighs over fifty tons (50,800 kg). Two smaller circles, each over 300 feet (91 m) in diameter, lie within the Great Circle. Only a few stones of the smaller circles survive.

Avebury is famous also for its alignments of standing stones, known as avenues. These avenues are two rows of stones that originally crossed the landscape for around one mile (1.6 km), joining the monument at its western and southern entrances. Little remains of either avenue.

STONE CIRCLES OF THE BRITISH ISLES

Stone circles are found in the north and west of the British Isles. More than nine hundred exist; some "circles" are actually oval-shaped. Many consist simply of a ring of standing stones, some less than fifty feet (15 m) across. Others, such as Avebury, are many times this size. They were built in the period between about 3500 and 1700 BCE.

The Purpose of Avebury

There can be little doubt that Avebury had a purpose, but what it was and how Avebury was used are mysteries. It seems to have been in use for some seven hundred years, when it may have acted as a focal point for people from a large area of southern Britain who gathered there at certain times of the year. Maybe visitors walked along the two avenues, using them as processional routes, before they entered the enclosure. No one knows what happened within the enclosure, but most experts believe that ceremonies were held there. These may or may not have been religious in nature.

SEE ALSO

• Prehistory • Stonehenge

▼ *The extent of Avebury's size can only really be appreciated from the air. Part of the encircling bank and ditch, and two of the four entrances can be seen. Within them lie the three stone circles, none of which are now complete. The village within the enclosure dates from the Middle Ages.*

◄ *A stone from the Beckhampton Avenue at Avebury, uncovered in 1999. Many of the stones of this alignment, including this one, had been toppled over and buried in pits in the Middle Ages.*

Babylon

During the second and first millennia BCE, Babylon was one of the most important cities in the ancient world. It stood on the banks of the Euphrates River some sixty miles (96 km) southwest of modern-day Baghdad in Iraq. Much of the city was unearthed by German archaeologists, led by Robert Koldewey, in the years from 1899 to 1914.

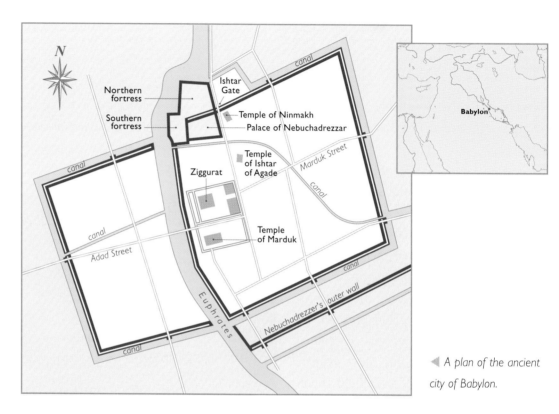

◀ A plan of the ancient city of Babylon.

City Walls

At the height of its glory, between 625 and 562 BCE, Babylon was the world's biggest city, covering an area of ten thousand acres (4,047 hectares). It was surrounded by double walls some thirteen miles (21 km) long. A Greek historian, Herodotus, described the outer walls as being 320 feet (97 m) high and 80 feet (24 m) thick – wide enough to allow a horse-drawn chariot to turn around on. Although modern historians doubt the accuracy of Herodotus's measurements, they agree that the battlements were certainly impressive. The bricks were covered in white glaze and decorated with images of roaring lions. Huge towers allowed guards to keep watch for invaders. A deep moat made it difficult for unwanted visitors to storm the gates.

The Gate of Ishtar

Babylon is the Greek form of Bab-ili, which means "the gate of God," and the city boasted no less than eight main gates. In his book *The Histories*, Herodotus claims the gates were "all of bronze with bronze uprights and lintels." The most spectacular of the entrances was the Ishtar Gate, dedicated to the Babylonian goddess Ishtar. It was decorated with rows of bulls and also of dragons – the symbol of the main

Babylonian god, Marduk. A special avenue ran through the gate, connecting a plaza outside the city with a temple complex inside. The avenue was built high above street level and paved with slabs of polished limestone trimmed with red rock. The walls on either side of it were decorated with huge images of lions and dragons moulded in relief on glazed bricks.

Temples and Palaces

The Euphrates River ran straight through Babylon, dividing it into two districts. On the east bank was the old city with its magnificent palaces and temples. On the west bank stood the new city, where most of the people lived. In the middle of the city was an enormous stepped pyramid called a ziggurat. Its seven platforms were connected by stairs. They led up to a temple on the summit that could be seen from far outside the city. The ziggurat was known by the Babylonians as Etemenanki, meaning "the house of the platform of heaven and earth." This structure was the famous Tower of Babel mentioned in the Bible.

A dazzling palace stood at the northern side of the old city, where the Babylonian kings entertained foreign dignitaries. At some point stood the Hanging Gardens of Babylon, the fabled landmark that was considered to be one of the seven wonders of the world. Built on a series of stepped terraces, the hanging gardens presented a true spectacle to the onlooker.

Invading Armies

Alexander the Great conquered Babylon in 331 BCE. By then most of the great temples and the ziggurat had been destroyed by Persian invaders. Alexander hoped to rebuild Babylon, but he died before he could carry out his plans.

THE FOLLOWING WORDS WERE INSCRIBED ON THE EDGE OF EVERY PAVING STONE ON THE SACRED PATH:

Nebuchadrezzar, King of Babylon, son of Nabopolassar, King of Babylon, am I. The Babel street I pave with blocks of shadu stone for the procession of the great Lord Marduk. Marduk, Lord, grant eternal life.

▼ *The famous Ishtar gate was built around 580 BCE. It was made of bricks covered in a pale blue shiny glaze that acted as a background to rows of carved bulls and dragons.*

In 275 BCE Babylon's last inhabitants were moved to a new city. Babylon, once the proudest city in the world, was left to fall into ruin.

THE HANGING GARDENS OF BABYLON

*P*hilo of Byzantium, a writer born around 250 BCE, had this to say about the Hanging Gardens of Babylon: "The Hanging Garden has plants cultivated above ground level, and the roots of trees are embedded in an upper terrace rather than the earth. The whole mass is supported on stone columns. Streams of water emerging from raised sources flow down sloping channels … the grass is permanently green and the leaves of the trees grow firmly attached to the supple branches. This is a work of art, a royal luxury and its most striking feature is that the work of cultivation is suspended above the spectators' heads."

▼ An eighteenth-century artist's impression of what Babylon might have looked like at the height of its powers. The Tower of Babel can be seen in the distance. In the foreground is the River Euphrates.

According to legend, King Nebuchadrezzar II constructed the Hanging Gardens for his wife around 600 BCE, but did they really exist? The Babylonians themselves left no written record of them. Some historians have suggested that the Hanging Gardens were actually at another city to the north, called Nineveh, which Greek and Roman sources often confused with Babylon. So far, the gardens remain undiscovered.

SEE ALSO
• Babylonians
• Ishtar • Marduk

Babylonians

The Babylonian culture flourished in southern Mesopotamia, a vast stretch of fertile land between the rivers Tigris and Euphrates. The Babylonians, a mixture of different tribes who spoke a Semitic language, twice built a dazzling empire. Influenced by the earlier Mesopotamian civilization of the Sumerians, their civilization began around 2200 BCE and ended in 539 BCE.

Babylonian Society

Babylonian society was divided into three classes. At the top were the nobility, known as the *amelu*. This class included the priests and military leaders as well as government officials, rich landowners, and wealthy traders. Below them were the *muskinu* (the commoners), who included craftsmen, builders, market traders, clerks, and farmers. The lowest class was the *ardu*, who were the slaves. In some ways, however, the law was harsher on the upper classes than on the lower ones because they were expected to set an example to society.

Slavery

Like many cultures of its time, Babylonian society was built on the use of slaves. Slave markets were very popular. Rich people went to the markets to buy prisoners of war. Sometimes poor citizens sold their children into slavery to pay off their debts.

Not all slaves were treated badly. Many were allowed to earn money in their spare time. Some were even allowed to have slaves of their own. If slaves could raise enough money, they were allowed to buy their freedom. Many slaves borrowed money to set themselves free.

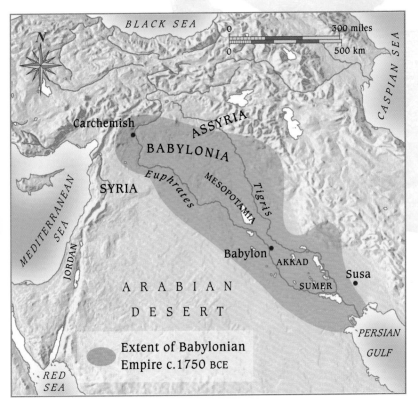

◀ The Babylonian empire in the time of Hammurabi (1792–1750 BCE).

Women

Babylonian women could be judges, elders, and witnesses to the signing of important documents. Some worked in the markets, selling goods like wine and grain. Even at the height of Babylonian civilization, however, women were considered much less important than men.

A girl was seen as the property of her father. When she came of age, he sold her to a future husband of his choice. During the wedding ceremony, the father handed his daughter a bridal gift, which she took with her to her new home. The gift was her dowry and remained hers, not her husband's, for the rest of her life.

A husband was expected to be faithful to his wife. If she could not have children, however, the wife might give him one of her slaves to produce heirs. Slaves who bore children for their masters were considered free women by law. Their children were legitimate. A woman could divorce her husband if he was cruel to her. In these circumstances, she could retain her dowry.

Food

The people of ancient Babylon made bread from barley and emmer, a form of wheat. They also grew millet and rice. Oil was extracted from sesame seeds, which were also used in baking. Onions and garlic were often used to add flavor to Babylonian dishes. Garlic and millet were grown in the king's gardens. Roasted goat and sheep were popular, as were wildfowl and fish caught in the Euphrates. Dates from the famous Mesopotamian palms were eaten raw.

▶ This relief, which decorated King Ashurnasirpal II's throne room in his palace at Nimrud, shows servants preparing meat for an Assyrian king's meal. Only rich Assyrians could afford to eat meat on a regular basis. Their professional cooks flavored it with wild herbs before roasting it.

BABYLONIANS

c. 2200 BCE

Rise of the Babylonian culture.

1792–1750 BCE

Reign of King Hammurabi.

c. 1590–1155 BCE

Babylon becomes the capital of Babylonia.

689 BCE

Sennacherib, king of the Assyrians, destroys Babylon.

614–612 BCE

King Nabopolassar puts an end to the Assyrian empire. Babylon enters its most glorious phase.

605 BCE

Nebuchadrezzar II becomes king of Babylon.

539 BCE

The Persians conquer Babylon.

331 BCE

Alexander takes control of Babylon.

275 BCE

The inhabitants of Babylon are moved to a new city. Babylon falls into ruins.

Trade

The Babylonians engaged in many different kinds of trade. They were gifted metalworkers. They produced leather goods, softening the leather with pulped animal brains. Bees were bred for honey, and lotus and lily flowers were grown to be crushed for perfumes.

Being in a fertile place, ancient Babylon was also renowned for its agriculture. Merchants from other countries came to trade their own goods for Babylonian crops. Ethiopians brought gold and ivory, while Arabs traded perfumes and aromatic oils. The Babylonians bought raw materials for their crafts, especially cedar, which they prized above all other woods.

Canals

It hardly ever rained in Babylon. The Babylonians depended on the Euphrates to water their crops. They constructed a complicated system of canals to irrigate the land around Babylon and managed to turn the desert into fertile ground. Officials were appointed to look after the canals. They had to make sure they were cleaned often to keep them free of weeds and reeds. King Hammurabi, who ruled possibly from 1792 to 1750 BCE, considered the canals so important that he personally ordered his governors to dredge them every time they became blocked. Neglecting a canal was regarded as a serious offense.

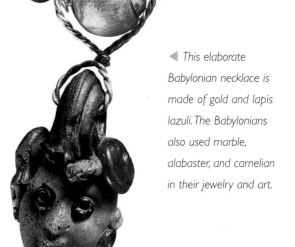

◄ This elaborate Babylonian necklace is made of gold and lapis lazuli. The Babylonians also used marble, alabaster, and carnelian in their jewelry and art.

ERISHTI-AYA, A YOUNG WOMAN LIVING IN A BABYLONIAN TEMPLE, WRITES TO HER FATHER COMPLAINING ABOUT LIFE IN THE TEMPLE:

The daughters of your house ... are receiving their rations of grain, clothing, and good beer. But even though I alone am the woman who prays for you, I am not provisioned.

Transport

Donkeys were perhaps the commonest form of transport in Babylon. They were used to carry goods to places as far away as Turkey, Armenia, and Syria. Carts pulled by donkeys or oxen were used to transport food and goods.

Boats were used for travel and transportation along the many canals and rivers of Babylon. River boats were usually made of reeds and covered with tar to make them waterproof. They floated downriver with the current but had to be pulled by donkeys or people when traveling the other way.

Architecture

As stone was scarce in ancient Babylon, wood and mud bricks were used to build most houses. Rich people lived in houses up to three stories high. The houses had flat roofs of dry mud, which were carefully sealed to keep out the rain. The very rich had bathrooms. These were usually at the southern end of the house. Water for washing was fetched from the river by slaves. Poorer people lived in round huts made of mud and reeds. The roofs of these huts were supported by central posts.

The streets of Babylon were built in a grid, creating square blocks of houses. Most streets were very narrow and ran parallel to the river. People dumped all sorts of rubbish in the streets. Every so often, workers would cover the rubbish with a layer of clay. Over the years, the streets rose higher and higher. Some people had to build steps that led down from the street to their front door.

▼ *Precious cedar wood is transported across water for use in the building of a royal palace in the city of Dur Sharrukin, in present-day Iraq. This eighth-century BCE stone relief was found in the ruins of the palace and is now in the British Museum.*

▲ Images of sacred animals, such as this bull, were used as decoration on the famous Ishtar Gate, the main entrance to Babylon itself. Above is a detail from a replica of the original gate, which can be found in Berlin, Germany.

Gods and Goddesses

Some of the Babylonian gods were inherited from the Sumerians, who had flourished in Mesopotamia before Babylonian culture began. Anu was the king of the gods, Ellil was the god of storms, and Ea was the god of wisdom and magic. The god of the city of Babylon was Marduk, who eventually came to be regarded as the supreme god of all the lands of the Babylonian Empire.

By at least 2000 BCE, Marduk – Ea's eldest son – was considered the main god in Babylon. The people called him Bel, meaning "Lord." Each year, during a festival, the statue of Marduk was carried out of his temple, known as the Esagila, to a place in the country. There the king himself came to receive his powers from Marduk.

HAMMURABI
REIGNED 1792–1750 BCE

Hammurabi was a great Babylonian king. He expanded his kingdom to include the city of Mari by the Euphrates. His empire was over seven hundred miles (1,126 km) long and one hundred miles (160 km) wide, the greatest Mesopotamia had seen until that time.

To keep control over his many subjects, Hammurabi drew up a list of 282 laws, which is known today as the Code of Hammurabi. The code dealt with many aspects of Babylonian life, including banking, wages, doctors' fees, divorce, the treatment of children, disputes between workers, and the punishment of criminals. One law stated that if a house fell down, its architect would be sentenced to death. Another decreed that if a man pulled out another man's eye, his eye should be poked out too. The code was carved on stone tablets and set up in many temples around the empire.

◀ King Hammurabi prays at a sacred tree in homage to Marduk. This gold and bronze statue, made in Babylon around 1750 BCE, was found in Larsa, southern Mesopotamia, and is now at the Louvre Museum in Paris.

This eighteenth-century BCE limestone tablet shows cuneiform writing. It describes how a canal was excavated in Babylon during the reign of King Hammurabi. Thanks to the hot climate of Mesopotamia, many examples of cuneiform writing have been preserved, though it is many centuries since Babylon fell to ruin.

CUNEIFORM

The Babylonians inherited the art of writing from the Sumerians. Their symbols were impressed on tablets of wet clay with a stylus. The clay was then hardened in the sun or baked until it set and the writing could not be erased. The symbols are made up of wedge shapes due to the use of a tip of a natural reed as a stylus. This form of writing is called cuneiform.

Ishtar was the goddess of physical love and war. She was represented by the planet Venus. Shamash was the sun god. The Babylonians believed that every morning he came out of a hill on the east side of the world. During the day he traveled across the sky till he arrived at another hill in the west. There, scorpion-men opened a huge door, and he disappeared through it. During the night he sailed by boat through the back part of the heavens to get to the east in time for sunrise.

The End of Babylon
Babylon had always prospered under strong kings. Its last rulers were weak, leaving the city prone to attack. In 539 BCE Babylon was conquered by the Persians under their king Cyrus the Great. In 331 BCE it was conquered again by the Macedonian king Alexander the Great, who died there. Alexander's followers founded Seleucia, a new city on the banks of the Tigris. The Babylonians were taken to live there, and their old city was abandoned.

SEE ALSO
• Astronomy • Babylon • Ishtar • Marduk • Marriage • Nineveh • Sumer

Bantu Culture

Bantu, meaning "the people," is the name given to a group of closely related languages that are spoken today over the whole of Africa south of the equator. The similarity of these languages over such a wide area suggests a common historical heritage. This theory is supported by the archaeological evidence for the period 500 BCE to 1000 CE, which shows the gradual southward spread of a common culture, marked by similar pottery, the presence of iron, and agriculture.

Bantu Migration

Historians believe that Africa south of the equator was gradually populated by immigrant Bantu speakers from the north, though there are no written records of early Bantu culture and very little in the way of physical remains for archaeologists to work on. In such a situation, tracing the movement of the Bantu language pro- vides an important clue when trying to follow develop- ments in the civilization of ancient Africa. It is known that at some stage the Bantu language split into two main branches, an eastern and a western branch, and in this divided form Bantu culture penetrated most of southern Africa, including Zimbabwe, Mozambique, Angola, Namibia, Botswana, and South Africa.

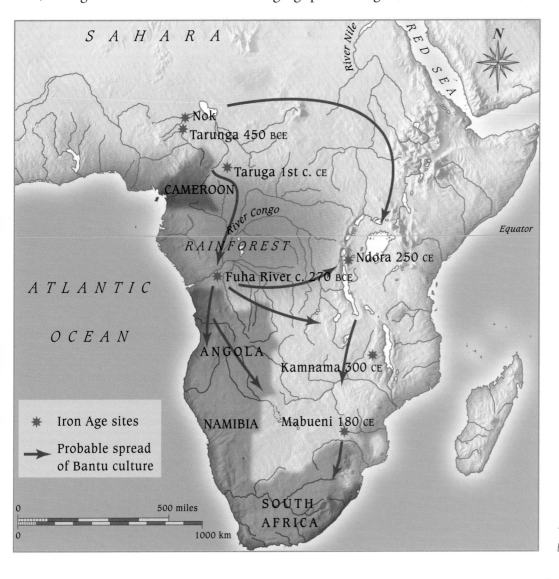

SAHARA

River Nile

RED SEA

N

Nok
Tarunga 450 BCE

Taruga 1st c. CE

CAMEROON

River Congo

RAINFOREST

Equator

ATLANTIC

OCEAN

Ndora 250 CE

Fuha River c. 270 BCE

ANGOLA

Kamnama 300 CE

NAMIBIA   Mabueni 180 CE

* Iron Age sites

→ Probable spread of Bantu culture

0   500 miles

0   1000 km

SOUTH
AFRICA

◀ The probable routes of Bantu migration.

These fragments of a pot, from Zambia in southern Africa, date from around the seventh century CE. By this time, Bantu culture was well established in southern Africa.

This iron projectile head from Zambia may have been part of a spear used in hunting or perhaps in warfare. It dates from the first millennium CE, a period when knowledge of iron making was spreading through southern Africa.

When the Bantu migration began, Africa south of the equator was cut off from the farming revolution that was transforming other parts of the world. The planting of crops and the rearing of domesticated animals changed the nature of food production in Egypt but had not penetrated southward. This lack of agriculture was due to the geography of central Africa, marked by areas of impenetrable rain forest and vast swamps around the equatorial source of the Nile.

Settled agriculture developed in southern Africa only around 500 BCE with the coming of the Iron Age. The Iron Age began in the Middle East around 1200 BCE and saw the gradual replacement of bronze weapons and tools by more easily produced and superior iron ones. Knowledge of ironworking had reached the Mediterranean coast of North Africa from the Middle East, and it gradually spread to west Africa along ancient trade routes across the Sahara Desert.

The Bantu migration may have helped the spread of knowledge about ironworking into central and southern Africa, although iron may not have been much used for tools until the end of the period, about a thousand years ago. Then, in what is called the Later Iron Age, there emerged a significant difference between the western and eastern branches of Bantu culture. In the west, the Bantu remained predominantly agricultural, but in the east, cattle keeping became very important.

Bantu Culture

Before the age of iron making, southern Africa was peopled by hunter-gatherer groups, dependent on hunting, fishing, and the gathering of wild plants for food. However, in parts of central Africa there were also settled communities that harvested wild plants and tended fruit trees, using stone tools crafted for the task. Gradually, Bantu culture caused a change in these methods of food production, although the original hunter-gatherers survived, together with their languages, as the so-called Bushmen of what is now Namibia.

Pastoralism – the keeping of domestic animals, like sheep and goats, for their milk and meat – existed in some parts of central and southern Africa before ironworking. Bantu culture helped introduce ironworking and settled forms of agriculture using cereal crops alongside any existing pastoralism. The spread of Bantu culture is also associated with the making of pots from clay. This process was an important technical development because pots

BANTU CULTURE

c. 500–100 BCE

Beginning of Bantu migration.

c. 200 BCE

Knowledge of iron-working begins to spread southward.

500 CE

Bantu culture is common across central and southern Africa.

▼ A woman in central Africa is learning to make pottery in much the same way as did her ancestors nearly two millennia earlier.

THE SPREAD OF BANTU CULTURE

The Bantu languages belong to the West African language group, so the original Bantu speakers probably lived in present-day eastern Nigeria and Cameroon. With the help of their simple agricultural culture, they seem to have moved through and around the equatorial forest into the more open country to the east and south to form two distinct groups, or "streams," of language and culture. In that more open country, their agriculture could flourish, leading to a considerable growth in population.

The earliest remains of settled agriculture and iron smelting in southern Africa date from the third and second centuries BCE, and over the next two centuries the eastern branch of Bantu culture spread southward into what is now South Africa. At the same time the western branch was moving into present-day Angola and Namibia.

affected how food was cooked and stored. In these ways Bantu culture marked the transformation of the hunting and gathering way of life.

Some Iron Age sites in central and southern Africa have been identified, and they point to the development of settled Bantu agricultural communities. These communities made pottery and decorated it with patterns, planted crops like millet and sorghum, and kept domesticated cattle and sheep. This way of life allowed the development of more settled societies.

By the end of the first millennium CE, the keeping of cattle and the storing of cereals became a visible form of wealth and power. A division between rich and poor emerged, leading to changes in ideas about the ownership of property and in turn to the idea of defending territory. A division also developed between men and women, with men tending and protecting cattle and thus acquiring a higher social status. Women devoted more of their time to farming land and preparing food.

This new way of life began to influence the hunting and gathering society that had existed before the arrival of Bantu culture. It was gradually adopted by the hunters and harvesters of wild plants. Until this change, they were still in an early stage of development, known as the Stone Age, when tools were all made from stone. Bantu culture established itself on a permanent basis as it slowly replaced this older way of life.

SEE ALSO

• Egypt • Nok Culture

CAUSES OF THE BANTU MIGRATION

The causes of the Bantu migration remain uncertain, but many anthropologists think it was caused by an increase in population. The harvesting of wild plants and tending of fruit trees developed into early forms of agriculture, and diets were further enriched by proteins and vitamins coming from improved means of fishing and the cultivation of palm fruits to make cooking oil.

As the population increased, people began seeking new lands to settle and cultivate. The pace of the Bantu migration may also have been influenced by the arrival of new plants in central Africa, like the vegetable banana called plantain, which could thrive in forest areas and close to rivers. Plants of the banana and yam families originally came from Indonesian islands lying to the east of Africa.

Belshazzar

Belshazzar, who reigned from 550 to 539 BCE, was the last ruler of the Babylonian Empire. His grandfather was Nebuchadrezzar II, the popular king who, according to legend, had built the Hanging Gardens of Babylon. Belshazzar's mother was a princess called Nitocris.

Nebuchadrezzar and Nabodinus

During his successful reign, Nebuchadrezzar had expanded the Babylonian Empire so that it stretched all the way from the Red Sea, across Mesopotamia and Syria, to Elam, a kingdom east of the River Tigris. In 604 BCE Nebuchadrezzar had also conquered the Hebrew city of Jerusalem, destroying its famous temple and, in 586 BCE, forcing the Jews into exile in Babylon.

Nebuchadrezzar's son and heir, Nabodinus, was not so successful. The Babylonians considered him weak. To make matters worse, Nabodinus preferred to worship the moon god, Sin, rather than the chief Babylonian god, Marduk. In 550 BCE the priests of Marduk led a revolt against him. Nabodinus fled to an oasis at Tayma, a cult center of the moon god in Arabia, leaving his eldest son, Belshazzar, to act as regent.

Belshazzar as Regent

Belshazzar not only had to govern his father's empire, he also had to manage his family's private estate and look after the Babylonian army. Like Nabodinus, he was not popular with his subjects, who considered him lazy and impious. During his eleven-year reign, there was famine in many parts of the empire.

Babylon Surrounded

Early in 539 BCE Cyrus the Great, king of the Medes and the Persians, surrounded Babylon with his armies. The Babylonians, trapped behind the city walls, prayed that their food supplies would not run out.

On October 12 Belshazzar held a great feast for all the noblemen in the city and their wives. According to the Book of Daniel in the Old Testament of the Bible, Belshazzar's rowdy guests drank out of the sacred goblets that Nebuchadrezzar had looted from the temple in Jerusalem. Many people, especially the Jews, considered this an act of sacrilege.

The Book of Daniel goes on to state that while the king and his friends were feasting, a hand appeared above Belshazzar. It wrote the words *Mene, Mene, Tekel, Parsin* on the wall. No one knew what these words meant. Queen Nitocris called for the Jewish prophet Daniel. He interpreted the inscription as an omen that Babylon was to fall to the enemy. Belshazzar was not fit to rule Babylon.

Belshazzar's Death

That same night, Cyrus's armies entered Babylon. The Greek writer Xenophon, describing Belshazzar's last stand in his book *Cyropaedia*, wrote how the king defended himself bravely with his sword. In the end he was cut down by Cyrus's two generals, Gobryas and Gadatas. Seventeen days later, Cyrus the Great himself entered Babylon to make it his winter residence. Belshazzar, the regent who had never quite become a king, became known as the man who lost the glorious Babylonian Empire.

> This is the interpretation of the thing: Mene; God hath numbered thy kingdom, and finished it. Tekel; Thou art weighed in the balances, and art found wanting. Peres; Thy kingdom is divided, and given to the Medes and Persians.
>
> DANIEL 5:26–28 (KJV)

SEE ALSO
- Babylon • Babylonians • Cyrus the Great • Hebrews
- Jerusalem • Marduk • Nebuchadrezzar II

▶ This seventeenth-century painting by Rembrandt shows King Belshazzar seeing the writing on the wall.

Book of the Dead

The Book of the Dead is the name given to writings put in tombs in ancient Egypt. At first only royal tombs were provided with these writings, which are known as Pyramid Texts, because they were written on the walls of burial chambers in some of the pyramids. As time passed, more and more people were buried with these writings. They were written on the inside of a person's coffin and were thus known as Coffin Texts.

A Guide to the Afterlife

The Book of the Dead was almost like a guide to the afterlife. It explains what the ancient Egyptians expected the afterlife to be like. To get to the afterlife, a person had to live a good life. The gods judged how well each person had lived by weighing the person's heart against a magical feather, the Feather of Truth. If a person had led a good life, the feather balanced perfectly with the heart.

A person who passed the test went to live in the Field of Reeds, which was just like ancient Egypt but perfect. The rivers were full of fish, the harvests were always good, and everyone was good-looking and healthy. If a person failed the test, a creature called Ammut, which had a crocodile's head, a lion's body, and a hippo's back legs, ate his or her heart. Without a heart, a person could not go to the afterlife.

Writing for the Dead

From around 1600 BCE the writings in the Book of the Dead began to be collected and copied out by scribes, the officials in ancient Egypt who could read and write. Writing was done on papyrus scrolls, which were long strips of a paperlike material made from reeds.

▼ This copy of the Book of the Dead was made for the scribe Hunefer in about 1300 BCE. From left to right, it shows Hunefer being led to judgment by the jackal-headed god of mummification, Anubis. Next, a smaller figure of Anubis balances Hunefer's heart against the Feather of Truth. The ibis-headed god of writing, Thoth, records the result. Hunefer passes the test, so the falcon-headed god Horus leads Hunefer into the presence of Osiris, god of the dead.

The scribes collected writings and drawings used in tombs and on coffins in earlier times. These drawings sometimes included maps of the afterlife, which the Egyptians thought of as being a physical place, like a country. These maps were usually drawn on the inside of coffins. The ancient Egyptians were the world's first mapmakers.

Different parts of the book were also copied out separately onto other objects buried in the tombs and onto the walls of the tombs themselves. For example, the ancient Egyptians buried mummy-shaped models of people in their tombs. These tiny people, called *shabti*s, were put in tombs to do the work of the dead person in the afterlife. *Shabti*s often had the part of the Book of the Dead that talked about work in the afterlife copied out on them.

Different Versions

Each copy of the Book of the Dead was made by hand for a particular person. While most of the text was the same in each case, there were differences where the text referred to the names and titles of the person it was made for. Some of the books are beautifully illustrated; others are not. The visual beauty of the book depended on how important the person was and how much the person or his or her relatives were able to spend on the copy.

SEE ALSO

- Death and Burial • Egypt
- Egyptian Mythology • Mythology

◄ *These shabtis were made for the priestess Henutmehyt in about 1290 BCE. The writing on the yellow part of the shabti, from the waist down, is part of the Book of the Dead.*

Boudicca

The mighty empire of ancient Rome suffered a humiliating defeat when Boudicca (c. 30–61 CE), a warrior queen, led a rebellion in Britain against the Roman invaders. Even though it was only a short-lived setback for their domination of western Europe, the rebellion's historian, Dio Cassius, described the events as a "terrible disaster."

The Tribes of Britain

When the Romans invaded Britain in 43 CE, it was not a unified country. The peoples who lived there belonged to many different tribal communities. Together they were known as the Celts. Each Celtic tribe lived within its own geographical territory. Some tribes, particularly those in south-eastern Britain, had traded with the Romans for many years and were friendly with them; these tribes welcomed the Romans. Others, however, opposed Roman rule.

Boudicca Against Rome

The east of Britain, where the present-day English counties of Norfolk and Suffolk are, was the tribal homeland of the Iceni. At first the leaders of this tribe were on good terms with the Romans. When their king, Prasutagus, died around the year 60, he left half his kingdom to Nero, the Roman emperor, and the other half to his wife, Queen Boudicca, and their two daughters. The Romans wanted all of it and set about taking Iceni territory and property by force. Worse still, the Romans flogged Boudicca and assaulted her daughters.

Boudicca took revenge. For several months, in 60 and 61, she led the Iceni and several other tribes with similar grievances, including the Trinovantes, in a rebellion against the Romans. Dio Cassius claims she led more than 100,000 troops, although this figure is probably an exaggeration.

▼ It is not certain what Boudicca really looked like. This illustration was made in the 1800s and is based on the description of her given by Dio Cassius.

Boudicca, Queen of the Iceni.

Boudicca's forces burned and destroyed the Roman towns of Camulodunum (Colchester), Londinium (London), and Verulamium (St. Albans). Some 70,000 civilians and Romans are said to have been killed by the rebels, and the Roman Ninth Legion suffered very heavy casualties. Prisoners were not taken.

The Romans Strike Back

At the time of Boudicca's rebellion, the Roman governor of Britain, Suetonius Paullinus, was engaged in a military campaign in north Wales, some 250 miles (400 km) away. When news of the revolt reached him, he marched south at the head of an army of ten thousand highly trained and well-armed Roman soldiers.

The site of the ensuing battle is not known, but it was a total victory for the Romans, who defeated the much larger but disorganized British force. Some 80,000 of Boudicca's followers – men, women, and children – were killed on the battlefield, against only 400 Roman dead.

Seeing that the rebellion had been crushed, Boudicca chose to end her own life. Both she and her two daughters took poison. According to Dio Cassius, Boudicca was buried with great honor, as befitted a queen and a hero. The Romans rebuilt the towns destroyed in the uprising, and the Celtic tribes of Britain had little choice but to accept that the Romans were there to stay.

▼ The large golden necklace that Dio Cassius says Boudicca wore was probably a torc, similar to one of these. Torcs were commonly worn by the Celts. They were symbols of wealth and power in Celtic society.

> In stature she was very tall, in appearance most terrifying, in the glance of her eye most fierce, and her voice was harsh; a great mass of the tawniest hair fell to her hips; around her neck was a large golden necklace; and she wore a tunic of many colors over which a thick mantle was fastened with a brooch. She shook a spear to terrify all who watched her.
>
> DIO CASSIUS, HISTORY OF ROME, BOOK 62

SEE ALSO

- Celts • Nero
- Roman Republic and Empire

Buddha

Buddha (c. 563–483 BCE) is the title given to Siddhartha Gautama, the spiritual leader who founded Buddhism, one of the world's great religions. The word *Buddha* means "the enlightened one" or "the awakened one." Buddha lived and taught in northern India. After his death, his followers spread the Buddhist faith to many parts of southern and eastern Asia and beyond.

Early Life

Most scholars believe Siddhartha Gautama lived from 563 to 483 BCE, but some claim he lived about a century later. He was born near the village of Lumbini in the foothills of the Himalaya mountains, on the border between India and Nepal. Siddhartha's father, Suddhodhana, was the local ruler and a Hindu prince of the Sakya clan. His mother, Maya, died soon after her son's birth, and so Siddhartha was brought up by his aunt.

Suddhodhana was a caring father, anxious about protecting his son from pain and hardship. The young prince grew up in the luxury of his father's palace. At the age of twenty, he married a local princess, Yasodhara. Soon the young couple had a baby son.

Siddhartha's Search for Truth

Having spent his whole life inside the palace, Siddhartha knew nothing of the poverty and sufferings of ordinary people. At the age of twenty-nine, however, he persuaded his charioteer to drive him beyond the palace walls. In the outside world Siddhartha met with suffering for the first time. He saw an old man bent double over his walking stick, a sick man suffering from a horrible disease, and a corpse being carried along in a funeral procession. Finally he saw a wandering holy man with yellow robes and a shaved head.

▼ The birthplace of Buddha is marked by this shrine in Lumbini, Nepal.

The suffering he saw filled the prince with horror and pity. He felt he could not continue with his former life but must set out on a quest to understand the reason for suffering in the world. One night he left the palace in secret, abandoning his wife and son. He cut off his long black hair, gave away his fine robes and jewelry, and set out with just a bowl so he could beg enough food to survive.

Siddhartha spent the next six years in the forests of northern India, learning from the Hindu teachers of his day. He lived a life of harsh self-denial, eating just one grain of rice a day, until his body grew very thin. Still he was no nearer to finding the answer to his quest. At last he decided to abandon the life of extreme self-discipline and take a middle course between luxury and denial. He continued his journey.

Understanding

Around 528 BCE Siddhartha's wanderings led him to the village of Bodh Gaya, near Bihar in northern India. There he resolved to sit in silent meditation under an ancient fig tree until he reached the understanding he sought. He sat cross-legged through the night. As dawn broke, he finally understood that suffering is caused by a person's own greedy desires and ignorance. Through this understanding he achieved nirvana, a state of peace and mental freedom. From then on, he was known as the Buddha, or Enlightened One.

Teachings

Soon after his enlightenment, Buddha began teaching. He gave his first sermon to five holy men at the deer park at Sarnath, near the city of Varanasi. The holy men became his first followers. Buddha's teaching, called the dharma, involves four principles, or Noble Truths. The first truth is that all life involves suffering; the second, that the cause of suffering is ignorance and attachment to worldly things; the third truth is that suffering will end when a person reaches the state of nirvana (blissful peace), which is beyond desire and selfishness; and the fourth, that nirvana can be achieved by living life in the correct way, according to a set of rules called the Noble Eightfold Path.

Buddha's Death and Beyond

Buddha spent the next forty-five years traveling the roads of northern India, teaching all who would listen to him, whether male or female, prince or beggar, young or old. At the age of eighty, he fell ill and died in a small town called Kusinagara. On his death he achieved an even fuller state of nirvana.

After Buddha's death his followers continued to spread his teachings. Some gave up their old lives to become monks and nuns. These followers were supported and fed by ordinary people. Over the centuries Buddhism gradually spread across India to the island of Sri Lanka, and then to Tibet, China, Korea, Japan, and many parts of Southeast Asia. It has become one of the world's most widespread religions, with followers in every region of the world.

▶ *This carving of Buddha's head comes from Sarnath in India, where Buddha began his teachings. It was carved in the fifth century CE.*

SEE ALSO

• Buddhism • Hinduism

BUDDHA DID NOT WRITE DOWN ANY OF HIS TEACHINGS HIMSELF. THE EARLIEST RECORDS OF HIS WORDS DATE FROM SEVERAL CENTURIES AFTER HIS DEATH. ONE EARLY TEXT RECORDS THE FOLLOWING WORDS OF ENCOURAGEMENT, WHICH BUDDHA IS SAID TO HAVE SPOKEN AT HIS DEATH:

Decay is found in all things. Live by making yourselves an island, your own refuge. Work toward Enlightenment with all your heart.

MAHAPARINIBBANA SUTRA

Buddhism

Buddhism is one of the world's major religions. It began in northern India during the sixth century BCE. In the centuries that followed, Buddhism spread southwards to Sri Lanka and Southeast Asia, northwards into Tibet, and east to China, Korea, and Japan. In all these countries different forms of Buddhism developed, depending on the existing beliefs and traditions. Buddhism has continued to spread in modern times.

Buddha

Buddhism was founded by a religious teacher, Siddhartha Gautama, who probably lived from 563 to 483 BCE. He is also known as the Buddha, a title that means "the enlightened one." Siddhartha was born a prince and lived a sheltered life until he was about thirty. At that age he encountered human suffering for the first time, in the form of sickness, old age, and death.

Siddhartha was so affected by this experience that he became a penniless monk, wandering in search of the meaning of life and the cause of suffering. After years of searching, he finally understood that all suffering is caused by human desire, greed, and ignorance. Sitting in meditation under a fig tree, he entered a calm, peaceful state called nirvana. At that moment he was enlightened and from then on was known as the Buddha.

Buddha was not content to rest after becoming enlightened. He wanted others to become enlightened, too. He founded an order of monks to spread his ideas. Buddha's teachings became known as the dharma, which means "law." The main ideas of Buddhism are summed up in sets of principles such as the Four Noble Truths and the Noble Eightfold Path.

The idea of reincarnation is central to Buddhist teaching, and many stories are told about the Buddha's own previous existences. Buddha taught that all living things are born, live, die, and are then reborn into another life in an endless cycle called samsara. He believed that the only way to break free of this cycle was to become enlightened.

The First Buddhists

The first Buddhists were people who heard Buddha preach and decided to change their lives as a result of his ideas. Some gave up their jobs to devote themselves to good acts and meditation (quiet, focused thought). They became monks and nuns, dependent on the kindness of ordinary people for shelter and food.

▼ This wall painting from a temple in Thailand shows a scene from Buddha's life. Prince Siddhartha cuts off his long black hair before setting out on his quest to find the cause of suffering in the world.

The first four principles of the Noble Eightfold Path are right understanding (of the causes of suffering), right thoughts (kind and compassionate thinking), right speech (not lying or criticizing others), and right action (harming no living thing and avoiding wrongful relationships and also drugs and alcohol). Next comes right livelihood (living honestly) and right effort (using energy in the right way). Finally Buddha urged his followers to practice right mindfulness (a person must be alert to what is going on inside and around him or her), and right concentration (a person should meditate to calm the mind and concentrate on whatever he or she is doing). Present-day Buddhists still try to live according to these ancient principles.

BUDDHIST BELIEFS

None of Buddha's teachings were written down in his lifetime. The first summaries of his ideas appeared about four hundred years after his death. Central to Buddhist thought is the idea that all living things suffer and that suffering is caused by attachment to worldly things. Buddhists believe that the only way to escape suffering is through enlightenment, a state that can be achieved by following a set of rules called the Noble Eightfold Path.

▲ This carving comes from a monument built by the Indian emperor Ashoka after his conversion to Buddhism. It shows Buddhists praying at the fig tree under which Buddha became enlightened.

India preaching. During Buddha's lifetime Buddhism spread rapidly through central India, sometimes replacing the ancient religion, Hinduism, and sometimes being practiced alongside it. After his death Buddhist monks began to carry his message to other countries.

Around 250 BCE the Indian emperor, Ashoka, became a Buddhist. He ordered pillars carved with Buddhist teachings to be set up all over India and also sent Buddhist missionaries abroad. The large island of Sri Lanka, south of India, was the first foreign land to accept the new religion. Later it became a Buddhist stronghold at a time when Buddhism in India itself was dying out.

Two Schools of Thought

During the first century CE a major split occurred among Buddhist thinkers. It led to the development of two distinct schools of thought: Theravada and Mahayana Buddhism.

Theravada is the older, more traditional form of Buddhism. The word *Theravada* means "way of the elders." Theravada Buddhists believed that people could attain enlightenment only through their own efforts. Thus, only a select group of monks and nuns who could devote their whole lives to Buddhism would achieve nirvana.

Mahayana Buddhists offered hope of enlightenment to a much larger group of people, including many who were not monks and nuns. They believed that certain enlightened beings, called bodhisattvas, would help others to become enlightened by delaying their own entry to nirvana. The word *Mahayana*, meaning "great vehicle," refers to this idea that more people would gain enlightenment through this school.

During his search for truth, Buddha had lived a life of harsh discipline and had almost died of starvation, but this path had not helped him to find nirvana, and so he preached a "middle way" to his followers, urging them neither to deny nor indulge themselves too much.

The Spread of Buddhism

After his enlightenment, Buddha lived for another forty-five years before dying at the age of eighty. He spent the last part of his life traveling about northern

Theravada was a simple form of Buddhism with few ceremonies. It became the main form practiced in Sri Lanka, later spreading to Myanmar (formerly Burma), Thailand, and other parts of Southeast Asia. Mahayana Buddhism developed a more complicated set of beliefs and rituals. Buddha had taught that he was not a god, simply an ordinary person whose teachings and example might help others. Nonetheless, Mahayana Buddhists came to think of Buddha and the bodhisattvas as divine.

▼ This shrine in southern Thailand was built to house Buddhist relics (remains) brought from Sri Lanka. The area became a major center for Buddhist worship during the third century BCE.

What we are today comes from our thoughts of yesterday, and our present thoughts build our life of tomorrow. . . . If a man speaks or acts with an impure mind, suffering follows him as the wheel of the cart follows the beast that pulls the cart. . . . If a man speaks or acts with a pure mind, then joy follows him as his own shadow.

THE DHAMMAPADA, C. 200 BCE

Buddhist beliefs gradually mixed with local customs and traditions to develop into many different forms of the one basic religion. In Tibet it mingled with the ancient religion of Bon-po. In China it mixed with the ideas of Confucianism and Daoism to produce many sects including Chan, which is known in Japan as Zen. After it spread to Japan, Zen was further influenced by the native religion of Shinto.

Buddhism has continued to spread since ancient times. During the twentieth century it attracted many new followers in Europe and North America, and it remains one of the world's most popular religions.

BODHIDHARMA
c.440–528 CE

Buddhism was carried from India to other parts of Asia by small bands of monk-missionaries. Many legends have grown up around these figures, including the one concerning Bodhidharma, an Indian monk who is credited with taking Buddhism to China in the fifth century CE. Bodhidharma is said to have founded Shaolin Monastery, which lies near the modern city of Zhengzhou in eastern China. At the monastery, legend says he encouraged the monks to perform special exercises to relieve their stiff joints after hours of sitting in meditation. The exercises developed into martial arts, for which the monastery became famous.

▲ A Buddhist monk prays as he walks around the Jokhang Temple in Lhasa, the Tibetan capital. The temple is said to have been founded around 650 CE, some five hundred years after Buddhism reached Tibet.

After the first century CE, Mahayanan Buddhism spread north across the Himalayas to Tibet. From there it was carried along the ancient trading route called the Silk Road to take hold in Mongolia, China, and Korea. By the sixth century CE it had reached Japan.

Different Kinds of Buddhism

Perhaps surprisingly, Buddhism did not remain the main religion in India, the country of its birth. It was gradually absorbed into the older religion of Hinduism. In many other countries

SEE ALSO
• Ashoka • Buddha • Chinese Philosophy
• Confucianism

Caesar, Julius

Julius Caesar (100–44 BCE) was a talented, ambitious Roman aristocrat and a brilliant military leader. His rise to power and eventual assassination led to the fall of the Roman Republic and the era of the emperors.

The Young Statesman

Determined to succeed in public and military life, Caesar became a governor in Spain in 61 BCE. This post had allowed him to build upon the military experience he had already gained, for example in the east between 80 and 78. In 59 he returned to Rome and forged an alliance with two Roman generals, Pompey and Marcus Crassus; this alliance is known as the First Triumvirate. Caesar was also elected consul (the leader of the Roman senate) for that year.

Conquest of Gaul and Crisis in Rome

Caesar spent the next nine years conquering Gaul (the area now occupied by France and Belgium). He also led an expedition to Britain in 55 BCE but did not attempt to conquer the country. The Gallic campaign ended in 50, when Caesar's legions defeated the Gaul leader, Vercingetorix, at the siege of Alesia. Meanwhile, Crassus was killed in battle, and Pompey became sole consul of Rome in 52 BCE.

▲ A bust of Caesar from the Vatican Gallery in Rome, clearly showing his stern expression.

CAESAR'S SENSE OF INJUSTICE AT HIS TREATMENT BY THE SENATE AT THE END OF THE GALLIC WAR IS CLEAR IN THIS EXTRACT FROM ONE OF HIS BOOKS:

Prestige has always been of prime importance to me, even outweighing life itself; it pained me to see the privilege conferred on me by the Roman people being insultingly wrested from me by my enemies. When I wrote to the senate suggesting a general demobilization, I was not allowed even that.

CIVIL WAR 1.9

The Death of Caesar by Vincenzo Camuccini. Caesar is said to have offered no resistance to the dagger blows; he pulled his toga over his head and fell to the ground. Afterward the conspirators ran through the streets, shouting "Liberty!" The citizens were horrified and disgusted.

Neither Pompey nor the senate wanted Caesar to become consul while still in command of such a large and experienced army. They insisted that Caesar give up his command. Caesar believed that doing so would make him vulnerable to his enemies, Pompey in particular. He wanted to avoid a slide into civil war between himself and Pompey, but he believed that the consulship should be his by right and felt insulted by the way he was being treated.

As a compromise, Caesar suggested that both of them give up their commands. However, the senators in Rome did not trust Caesar. They feared him and believed he was a threat to the republic. So they gave absolute power to Pompey in the hope that he could save them.

Crossing the Rubicon

By this time Caesar was at the River Rubicon, which marked the boundary between Gaul and Italy. He made a momentous decision and crossed into Italy with his army: an act of war. Pompey was forced to try and repel Caesar's armies. However, Caesar quickly overran Italy, and Pompey fled to Greece, where Caesar defeated him at Pharsalus, in northeastern Greece. Pompey escaped to Egypt, where he was later murdered.

Caesar and Cleopatra

Caesar pursued Pompey to Egypt, where he met Cleopatra. He was fascinated by the sixteen-year-old queen and delayed his return to Rome by several months. While

POMPEY THE GREAT
C.106–48 BCE

Pompey was a powerful Roman general who campaigned successfully in Spain in 77 BCE and with Marcus Crassus against Spartacus's slave revolt in 71 BCE. In 66 he campaigned in the east, defeating Mithridates, the king of Pontus (in Asia Minor). He was for a brief time married to Caesar's daughter, Julia. Many of Pompey's contemporaries felt that his undoubted military talent was overshadowed by his vanity. Caesar is said to have wept on hearing the news of Pompey's murder.

▼ As a young man, Pompey was said to be very handsome, even beautiful. By the end of his life, however, luxurious living in Rome had taken its toll on his looks.

in Egypt his army defeated Ptolemy, Cleopatra's brother and her rival for the Egyptian throne. There were rumors in Rome that Caesar was in love with Cleopatra, and she later claimed that Caesar was the father of her son, Caesarion, whom she named after him. However, Caesar had another reason for forging greater ties with Egypt and for securing the Egyptian throne for Cleopatra from her brother: Egypt was a wealthy nation and the main source of Rome's grain supply.

Dictatorship and Death

Victorious over Pompey, Caesar was made dictator and ruled for five years. During this brief period he carried out various reforms, including the introduction of a new calendar, but did nothing to provide for Rome's future. He was accused of acting like a king, a type of leadership most Romans were deeply opposed to. A conspiracy was formed to kill Caesar, led by Cassius and Brutus. He was stabbed to death in the senate house on March 15, 44 BCE.

Character

Julius Caesar was energetic, quick-witted, highly ambitious, and capable of total ruthlessness. Surviving statues show him as clean shaven, with a stern face and hair combed forward to cover his baldness. He is described as being a tall man with very dark eyes. His brilliance as a public speaker led Cicero to call him "the most eloquent of all Romans."

SEE ALSO

- Augustus • Calendars • Cicero
- Cleopatra • Roman Republic and Empire
- Spartacus

Calah

Calah (modern Nimrud), nineteen miles (30 km) south of present-day Mosul, was one of the main centers of ancient Assyria. Although known as Calah in the Old Testament of the Bible, the Assyrians themselves called it Kalhu. The site was well chosen, for the Tigris and Upper Zab Rivers protected the city to the west and south.

Shalmaneser I founded the Assyrian city of Calah around 1280 BCE upon the ruins of a much older town that dated back to at least the sixth millennium BCE. However, Calah's most glorious period came in the reign (883–859 BCE) of the great Ashurnasirpal II, who made the city the capital of his kingdom.

Construction of Calah

An inscription describes the banquet that King Ashurnasirpal gave to celebrate the foundation of his new palace at Calah in 879 BCE. He provided ten days of feasting, baths, and other luxuries for the city's population of 16,000 as well as for the ambassadors from neighboring countries; the number of party goers swelled to an estimated 69,000.

Ashurnasirpal also set out to construct a capital that showed off the might of Assyria. The outer wall was over five miles (8 km) in length and enclosed an area of 890 acres (360 hectares). The highest structure in the town was the ziggurat, a stepped pyramid. A canal was cut from the Upper Zab to irrigate the surrounding fields and safeguard the city's water supply in time of war. The canal was called Patti-hegali, meaning "the stream of abundance."

In time Calah became an important center of Assyrian religion. Of the nine temples constructed on the orders of Ashurnasirpal, three or four have been located. They were dedicated to Nabu, the god of writing; the goddess Ishtar; and Ninurta, the war god.

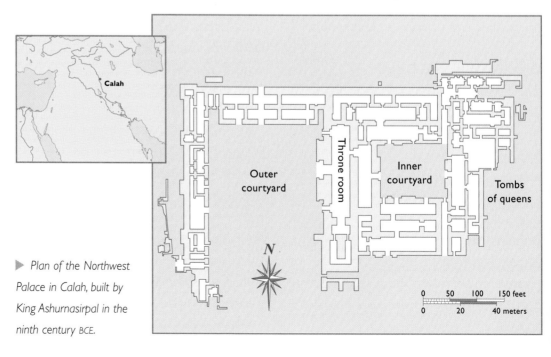

▶ Plan of the Northwest Palace in Calah, built by King Ashurnasirpal in the ninth century BCE.

The Northwest Palace

Ashurnasirpal II governed from his magnificent palace, known today as the Northwest Palace. The palace walls were decorated with stone bas-reliefs (shallow sculptures), which were highlighted with brightly colored paint. The timber came from red cedars and other woods felled on the slopes of the distant Amanus and Lebanon Mountains.

The inner courtyard was defended by giant stone statues of winged bulls with human heads that represented friendly supernatural beings who watched over the king. Weighing as much as sixteen tons (14,515 kg), the statues astonished the nineteenth-century archaeologists who first discovered them.

Decline

Calah ceased to be the capital of Assyria around 710 BCE, when the government moved to Dur Sharrukin (near modern Khorsabad), the city of King Sargon II. Calah may have been sacked twice by the Medes between about 614 and 612 BCE, when the Assyrian Empire collapsed. It then lay practically deserted for centuries.

▲ *The nineteenth-century British artist James Ferguson drew a reconstruction of Calah as he thought it may have been in Assyrian times. Although he based it on excavations carried out there, the drawing contains inaccuracies, such as the inclusion of Greek-style columns, which the Assyrians did not use.*

SHALMANESER III
REIGNED 858–824 BCE

Shalmaneser III reigned for thirty-five years. He spent thirty-one of them at war, so he spent little time at his capital of Calah. Yet he built a vast palace there that archaeologists have nicknamed Fort Shalmaneser. As well as the king's living quarters, the palace contained storehouses where supplies of every kind – chariots, horses, weapons, and foodstuffs – were gathered together by the Assyrian army. Shalmaneser also ordered the building of the so-called Black Obelisk, discovered by the British archaeologist A. H. Layard in 1845. This six-and-a-half-foot (2 m) high block of black alabaster is one of the most significant finds yet made in the territory of ancient Assyria.

SEE ALSO

• Assyrians • Ishtar
• Sargon of Akkad

Calendars

A calendar is a system that counts units of time – days, weeks, and years. Ancient societies, which depended on agriculture for survival, divided the years into seasons. The Egyptians had three seasons: the season when the Nile flooded its banks, spreading fertile mud over their fields, the season when they sowed their crops, and finally the harvest season.

The Year

The Egyptians were the first people who felt the need to measure time in more accurate units. As a religious society, they needed to know when to prepare for festivals and when to celebrate the births and deaths of the pharaohs. Astronomers had noticed that the Nile always flooded around the same time that the constellation Sirius and the sun rose in the sky together. They considered the time between these joint risings of Sirius and the sun to be one long unit – a year. Using the cycles of the moon, the Egyptians then divided the year into days, weeks, and months. There were 365 days in one Egyptian year, grouped into units of weeks and months.

By 3000 BCE the Chinese too had developed a calendar of 365 days. Around 2100 BCE the Mesopotamians were using two calendars, a lunar calendar, based on the cycles of the moon, and a solar calendar, based on the sun. The solar calendar had 360 days in it, the lunar calendar, only 354.

Months

The Egyptians divided the year into twelve months of thirty days each. At the end of the year, there were five days that belonged to no month. They were set aside for the gods' birthdays and a festival celebrating the coming of the new year and the flooding of the Nile, an event that made Egypt fertile. It is not known exactly how the Egyptians named their months until the sixth century BCE, when they were named after festivals.

Days and Weeks

The ancient Egyptians grouped the days into weeks of ten days each. Babylonian astronomers, however, believed the number seven to have magical properties. Their week had seven days. The ancient Jews adopted the custom; as it is written in the Old Testament of the Bible, God created the world in six days and rested on the seventh.

▼ A nineteenth-century illustration of Egyptians testing a Nileometer, a practice dating back to around 4000 BCE

The Romans used an eight-day week because most towns held a market every eight days. The practice was abolished in 321 CE, when the emperor Constantine introduced the seven-day unit used in the Old Testament. A convert to Christianity, Constantine decreed Sunday the first day of the week. It was to be a day of prayer.

▲ *The Maya used their knowledge of the stars to make predictions and to establish a calendar of 365 days. This calendar of predictions, compiled in the fourteenth century CE, showed which days of the year were good or bad.*

NAMING THE DAYS

The Babylonians named the days of the week after the planets they knew about in the solar system. The Romans adapted the names to their language. Monday was the moon's day; Tuesday, Mars's day. Wednesday, Thursday, Friday, and Saturday were named after Mercury, Jupiter, Venus, and Saturn, respectively. Sunday was named after the sun, which was worshiped as a god in ancient times. Some of these names, namely Sunday, Monday, and Saturday, are still in use.

The English names for the other days of the week came from the names of gods in northern European mythology. Tuesday was named after Tyr, the Norse god of war. Wednesday was named after Woden, or Odin, the god of wisdom. Thursday was the day of Thor, the god of thunder, and Friday was Frigg's day. She was the Norse goddess of love.

SOSIGENES OF ALEXANDRIA

Sosigenes was a Greek mathematician and astronomer living in Alexandria in Egypt during the first century BCE. When Julius Caesar wanted to change the calendar used around the Roman Empire, he chose Sosigenes to work out a new and more precise one. Caesar met the astronomer while he was in Egypt in 49 and 48 BCE. Cleopatra, the ruler of Egypt, and partner of Julius Caesar, almost certainly recommended Sosigenes herself.

Sosigenes wrote many works but only fragments of one book, called *Revolving Spheres*, survive. From his writings historians learned that the Greek astronomer correctly believed that the planet Mercury revolved around the sun.

Leap Year

The exact length of a year is 365 days, five hours and forty-eight minutes – about a quarter of a day longer than the Egyptian calendar had stated. The shortfall meant that, in ancient Egyptian times, the calendar would gradually get out of step with the seasons. By the time Julius Caesar became ruler of Rome in 46 BCE, it was three whole months behind the seasons. Caesar enlisted the help of Sosigenes, a Greek astronomer, to solve the problem and find one calendar that could be used all around the empire. Sosigenes added an extra day to the year every four years, thus creating the leap year. His calendar became known as the Julian calendar, after Julius Caesar.

SEE ALSO

- Astronomy • Babylonians • Caesar, Julius
- Constantine • Egyptians
- Roman Republic and Empire

◀ This tablet, carved around 500 BCE, was used by the ancient Babylonians to calculate Jupiter's movements through the skies. They believed Jupiter to be the god Marduk. Following the sacred star helped them keep an accurate track of time.

Caligula

The name of Caligula, who lived from 12 to 41 CE, has traditionally been associated with self-indulgence, cruelty, and madness. His reign as emperor of Rome lasted less than four years.

Hopeful Beginnings

Caligula's real name was Gaius Caesar Augustus Germanicus. Caligula was a nickname, meaning "little boot." It was given to him by Roman soldiers when he was a child because he wore shoes that were similar to a legionary's *caliga*, a sandal or boot.

Caligula was the great-nephew of the emperor Tiberius, who named him as his heir. Caligula became emperor in the spring of 37 CE, two days after the death of Tiberius. Romans were at first delighted to have a new, young emperor. Tiberius, despite having kept the empire stable over a reign of twenty-three years, had been seen as a miser and was very unpopular among the common people. Caligula made a promising start, abolishing taxes and vowing to cooperate with the Roman senate.

Illness

Six months into his reign Caligula fell seriously ill. He may have suffered a nervous breakdown or been afflicted by epilepsy, no one can be sure. Whatever the cause, when he recovered in November 37, he was a changed man. He became increasingly afraid of plots against him and began ordering the execution of anyone he suspected of disloyalty. His fondness for lavish living increased, and he began to raise money by confiscating land and property.

▶ *A marble bust of Caligula held in the Louvre, Paris. The sculptor has been kind to the emperor: images of Caligula on coins, as well as contemporary descriptions, suggest he was an ugly man.*

Caligula left Rome in September 39. His intention was to conquer Britain. The expedition failed owing to poor discipline and organization in the army. The army never left the coast of northern France.

End Game

In the final months of his brief reign, Caligula apparently believed himself to be a god and talked to statues of Roman gods as if he were their equal. Whether this was true madness or an example of his dark sense of humor will never be known. However, a plot was hatched to murder him, and he was stabbed to death in January 41. His wife and daughter were killed later the same day. Caligula's name was then removed from official records, and his statues were pulled down.

Fairly Remembered?

Caligula's reign is full of contradictions. Was he mad, or was his odd sense of humor distorted by his enemies to make him appear mad? He certainly spent a great deal of money on lavish living, but he cannot have drained the state funds dry, because Claudius, his successor, found them quite healthy when he became emperor. Although Caligula had lost the support of the senate by the end of his reign, the common people were angry at his murder. The truth is that Caligula was probably far too young and inexperienced to cope with the pressures of being emperor. Perhaps history's judgment of him has been too harsh.

SEE ALSO

• Claudius • Roman Republic and Empire
• Rome, City of

▼ *Caligula loved chariot racing and spent huge sums on horses. He even had his own private race track on his estate.*

Carthage

One of the most powerful empires of ancient times, Carthage was a city-state built on a peninsula on the shores of what is now called the Gulf of Tunis, part of modern-day Tunisia. At its height, between the late sixth century and the third century BCE, Carthage was the richest city in the world, with colonies along the coast of North Africa, in Sicily, and in southern Spain. Its wealth and power were built on trade, especially in gold, silver, tin, and iron.

History

Legend says that Carthage was founded by a Phoenician princess named Dido in 814 BCE, but archaeology suggests that its founding was actually one hundred years later. By the fifth century BCE Carthage controlled most of what is now Tunisia, where the conquered people were forced to pay tribute and provide soldiers for the city-state.

In 480 BCE Carthage went to war with the Greek city of Syracuse on the island of Sicily and was heavily defeated. Carthage remained in control of the west of the island but from the end of the fifth century BCE waged a series of wars with the Greeks for control of Sicily. In the third century BCE the powerful city-state of Rome was drawn into the conflict on the side of the Greeks. In three major wars (264–241, 218–201, and 149–146 BCE) the Romans first drove Carthage out of Sicily, then took all its European colonies, and finally attacked and destroyed the city.

▼ These excavated ruins show part of the city of Carthage on the Hill of Byrsa, where the citadel was built.

DIDO

Roman legends tell that Dido, the daughter of the king of Tyre and the wife of a fabulously wealthy merchant, fled from her home after her brother, Pygmalion, had murdered her husband. She took with her all her husband's vast wealth in silver and gold and landed on the coast of Africa, where she asked the native people for some land to build a settlement. They laughingly told her she could have as much land as she could cover with a cow hide. She and her followers carefully cut the hide into tiny strips and used it to mark out the hill on which the citadel of Carthage was built. According to legend many years later she chose to build her own funeral pyre and stab herself to death as she lay on it.

▼ This mosaic shows the figure of a woman known as the Lady of Carthage and is from the sixth century CE, when Carthage had become a Christian city.

Culture

Carthaginian culture was Phoenician in origin. Carthaginians worshiped a supreme being called Baal Hamon and a goddess called Tanit. Their religious practice involved human sacrifice of children. The artwork of the Carthaginians was at first simple and sketchy but became more elaborate under the influence of Egyptian and especially Greek art. No literature has survived, nor do ancient sources, such as the Roman writers, mention any. The language spoken in Carthage was a form of the ancient language of the Phoenicians. It had a written form that survives only as inscriptions on gravestones. It consisted only of consonants.

The City

Carthage was a walled city. Its walls extended twenty-two miles (35 km) around the peninsula and were forty feet (12 m) high and thirty feet (9 m) thick on the landward side. It had two artificial harbors, and on the hill above, there was an inner wall around the citadel. Houses had flat roofs and no outer windows, but each one enclosed a private courtyard.

SEE ALSO
• Aeneid • Hannibal • Phoenicians

Çatal Hüyük

Çatal Hüyük is an archaeological site in south-central Turkey, once home to an advanced Neolithic (later Stone Age) culture. British archaeologists working there from 1961 to 1965 uncovered buildings and artifacts that added important new information to what is known of Neolithic culture. Excavated buildings at Çatal Hüyük date approximately from 6500 to 5500 BCE, and the area of the site is thirty-two acres (8.5 hectares).

Farming and Trade

During the early Neolithic period people first began to plant crops and rear domestic animals. Before Çatal Hüyük was excavated (Hüyük is the Turkish word for an ancient settlement mound), it was believed that this revolution in farming took place to the east in what is now Iraq and the eastern Mediterranean. The finds at Çatal Hüyük proved that Neolithic culture had spread farther to the west.

Çatal Hüyük lived by farming and hunting. The community grew and harvested crops, including flax, and probably kept animals as well. The people of Çatal Hüyük also engaged in trade with other communities. Indications of trade come from finds of seashells at this inland site and evidence of nonlocal metals. Çatal Hüyük helped spread the Neolithic farming revolution westward into Europe.

Houses

The houses at Çatal Hüyük were built using handmade bricks dried by the sun. The houses had shared walls, and each house was built around the sides of others. The entrance to each house was perhaps by way of a common flat roof. It is likely that the large roof provided a communal area for the inhabitants of the houses. Ladders were used to access the rooms below.

◀ Located well inland, Çatal Hüyük was a Neolithic farming and hunting community. Archaeological evidence of widespread trading activity has been uncovered.

The rooms in each house were of similar design. The town had no streets, and this tightly packed architecture provided a form of defense, although no wall was built around the settlement.

Artifacts

A variety of artifacts excavated at the site provide evidence of the highly developed culture of Çatal Hüyük. Pottery has been discovered there, some of which is crude and undecorated. However, the likelihood that it could be nine thousand years old makes it the earliest known pottery in the world. More elaborate pottery has also been found, as well as decorated bone tools and small figures of humans shaped from stone and clay. Other spectacular finds include actual fragments of textiles – the oldest found on any archaeological site – that were preserved in the dry soil along with small vessels shaped from wood and parts of implements from spinning and weaving appliances.

SEE ALSO

• Farming • Jericho

NEOLITHIC ART

Some of the rooms at Çatal Hüyük were decorated in special ways that suggest they were not ordinary living or sleeping quarters. For example, some shrinelike rooms were adorned with the skulls and horns of animals, as well as plaster copies. Wall paintings in other rooms featured hunting scenes and aspects of ordinary Neolithic life. These paintings provide invaluable evidence of how the inhabitants dressed and show some of their activities. Other wall paintings featured designs with patterns that correspond in some ways to the cave paintings of the Paleolithic age, a more primitive period, when people were hunters and gatherers, and used unpolished stone tools.

▼ A wall painting from Çatal Hüyük, dating from the seventh millennium BCE, shows animals and dancing people.

Celts

The Celts were a group of fierce warriors, talented engineers, and art lovers who emerged around 1200 BCE. They were the earliest and greatest Iron Age civilization. By 700 BCE the Celts were producing iron in large quantities. From their homes in the center of Europe, they spread outwards. Within a few hundred years there were Celtic tribes in every corner of Europe. Even today, in places as far apart as Ireland, Spain, and Turkey, people can still find traces of the ancient Celts in their art, their language, and even in their genes.

As they spread across Europe, the Celts separated into a great number of different tribes, such as the Nervii of northern Gaul (modern Belgium). The tribes continued to share a language, a religion, and customs, even though they grew geographically separate. The ancient Celts loved listening to stories and music, but they did not leave any written records. However, as they moved around, they continued to make their unique iron tools and their decorated weapons, and archaeologists have been able to piece together their history from the objects they have left behind.

Early History

The earliest Celts were a group of people living around 1200 BCE. Their culture is called the Urnfield Culture because they cremated their dead and put the ashes in urns, which they buried in fields. Over the next few hundred years small groups started to break away and settle in different parts of Europe. The central group of Celts stayed in the same area, spreading west and south, sometimes fighting against other Celts. By 700 BCE they covered a much wider area and were masters at using iron.

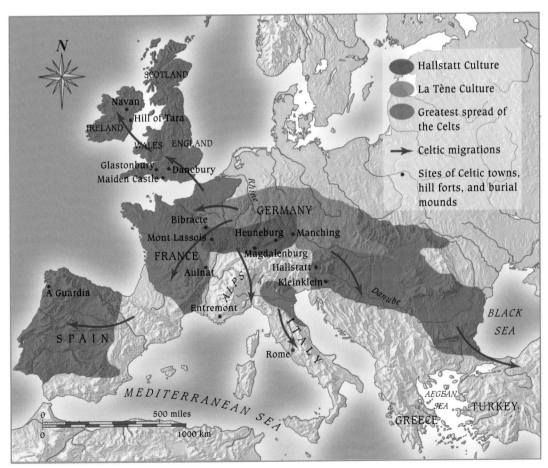

◀ As the map shows, the Celts moved across virtually the entire extent of Europe.

The Celts became very rich from controlling the traffic along the rivers in their area and from trading with the Greeks to the south. This period, starting around 750 BCE, is called the Halstatt Culture, after a town in Austria where a great number of their ingenious iron tools and weapons have been found.

The Invasions

In 400 BCE a tribe called the Etruscans was living in the lush Po Valley in northern Italy. The Etruscans had never heard of the Celts when they swept down over the Alps from the north, conquered the Etruscans, and took their land. Next the Celts marched south to Rome and besieged the city. The Romans had to pay them a vast sum of gold to get them to leave. The Celts settled to the north of Rome in a territory the Romans called Cisalpine Gaul. Here and all over Europe the Celts enjoyed a long period of domination. However, one by one, the various Celtic tribes were conquered by Greek and Roman armies. Gradually Celts started to intermarry with local cultures, and Celtic identity began to disappear.

The Roman Empire

By 192 BCE the Roman Empire had conquered Cisalpine Gaul. Blocking the path of further Roman expansion to the north was the final Celtic stronghold in continental Europe, called Transalpine Gaul. By 57 BCE Julius Caesar had succeeded in conquering it, and he was able to declare that all the Celts in Gaul were Roman subjects. In 43 CE the Romans arrived in Britain, another land where Celtic tribes had established themselves. Over the next forty years the Romans advanced north, defeating the tribes that had settled there. By the end of the first century CE, most of Britain was Romano-Celtic.

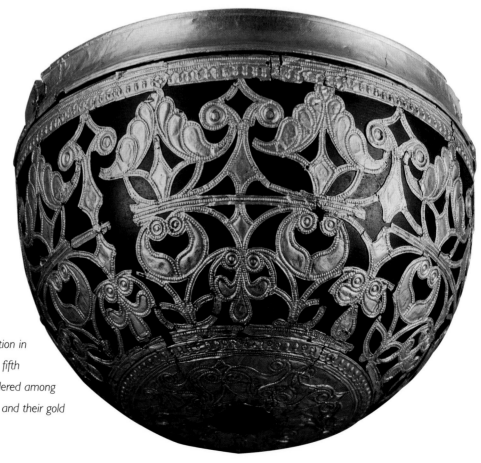

▶ A Celtic bowl with gold decoration in the La Tène style, dating from the fifth century BCE. The Celts were considered among the best craftspeople of their day, and their gold work was highly valued.

CELTS

1200 BCE

Urnfield Culture, central Europe.

500 BCE

La Tène Culture, Switzerland.

276–279 BCE

Celtic tribes defeated in Greece.

57 BCE

Caesar conquers all of Gaul.

430 CE

Anglo-Saxons start invading Britain.

750 BCE

Halstatt Culture, Austria.

400 BCE

Invasion of Italy.

192 BCE

Rome conquers Cisalpine Gaul.

84 CE

Nearly all of Britain under Roman rule.

432 CE

St Patrick converts the Irish Celts to Christianity.

CELTIC ARTS AND CRAFTS

The Celts decorated almost everything they made, from swords and shields to boxes and mirrors. The basis was iron, and they added bronze, semiprecious stones, colored enamels, and sometimes gold and silver. The most famous examples of Celtic art were made by Celts of the La Tène Culture. This group of Celts emerged in Switzerland in 500 BCE, and soon their artistic style was found all over Europe. It involves surfaces filled with curves, swirls, spirals, circles, and floral designs. The patterns are often symmetrical and always abstract – La Tène style almost never depicted people or animals.

Celtic Ireland

During the fifth century CE Britain was invaded by the Anglo-Saxons, but the Celts remained in the edges of Britain, in Cornwall, Wales, and Scotland. An early Christian called Patrick took a group of Celts to Ireland and established a church there. Ireland became the cultural center of Celtic Christianity. Modern-day Irish people still speak a Celtic language and are very conscious of their Celtic roots, as are some people in Scotland and Wales, and Brittany in northern France.

▶ *A piece of bronze jewelry with bell pendants, dating back to the La Tène culture.*

Maiden Castle in southwest England is the biggest Iron Age hillfort in Europe. Its interior covers more than sixty acres (25 ha). The first earthwork built on the site was Neolithic, dating back to about 4000 BCE.

Celtic Society

The Celts grew grains, which they traded with the Romans, but they were primarily cattle farmers. The Celts were an innovative people. They developed techniques for keeping bees and curing hams. They also invented a crude compass, a pottery wheel, and a rotary millstone. Their clothes were very brightly colored.

The Celts had a strong sense of social hierarchy. Each tribe had an elected chieftain. The next most important people were the druids, the tribe's highly trained priests. They also acted as judges, doctors, and philosophers. Other social classes were the bards (who sang songs and told stories), the warriors, and the farmers.

The Celts worshiped many gods and made human sacrifices to them. They believed the soul was immortal and passed into another body after death. Mistletoe was sacred to the Celts, especially when it grew on an oak tree. Many of their religious ceremonies took place at stone altars in oak forests. As Celtic tribes were absorbed into the local cultures of the lands in which they settled, their druidic religion died out.

They are very tall in stature, with rippling muscles under clear white skin. Their hair is blond ... they bleach it ... artificially, washing it in lime and combing it back from their foreheads. They look like wood-demons, their hair thick and shaggy like a horse's mane. Some of them are clean shaven, but others ... shave their cheeks but leave a moustache that covers the whole mouth and, when they eat and drink, acts like a sieve, trapping particles of food.

DIODORUS SICULUS, A GREEK HISTORIAN OF
THE FIRST CENTURY BCE

SEE ALSO

- Etruscans
- Roman Republic and Empire

Chang'an

Chang'an was an important city in ancient China. It served as the capital for several dynasties of Chinese rulers. The modern city of Xi'an in the Shaanxi Province of northern China now stands on the site of the old city of Chang'an.

History of the City

The area around Chang'an has been settled since Neolithic times, about six thousand years ago. From around 1100 to 450 BCE Zhou kings ruled northern China from their capital at Hao. In the late third century BCE China's first emperor, Cheng, built a new capital, Xianyang, nearby. After Cheng's death his dynasty, the Qin (or Ch'in), was ended by a soldier named Liu Bang, who became Emperor Gaozu, first in a new dynasty of Han rulers. Han emperors controlled China for the next four hundred years. Cheng had been a harsh ruler who did not like criticism. Gaozu ruled less sternly than his predecessor.

As had become customary, Gaozu built a new capital to mark his reign. In an optimistic mood he called it Chang'an, which means "eternal peace."

Like other Chinese cities, Chang'an was well defended. It was enclosed by stout walls up to sixty feet (18 m) high and fifty feet (15 m) thick. The gates leading into the city were shut and guarded at night. Much of the southern and central city was occupied by royal palaces and government offices. The rest was divided into areas called wards. Craftsmen and the emperor's servants lived in the northwest, while other citizens lived in the northeast.

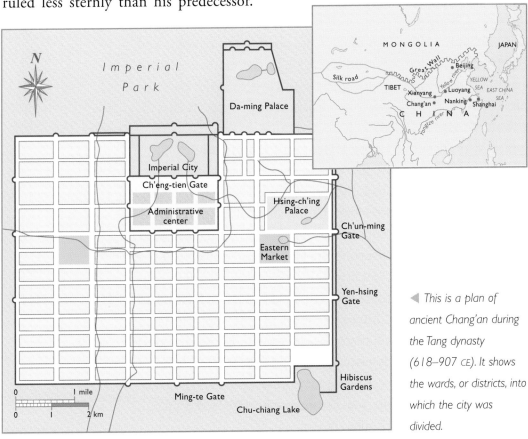

◄ This is a plan of ancient Chang'an during the Tang dynasty (618–907 CE). It shows the wards, or districts, into which the city was divided.

◀ This eighteenth-century painting shows Liu Bang, who became the Emperor Gaozu and founded the Han dynasty.

EMPEROR GAOZU
256–195 BCE

Emperor Gaozu, the first Han ruler, began life as a humble official named Liu Bang in the service of the Qin emperor Cheng. When Cheng died, Liu Bang led a peasant uprising against the harsh Qin dynasty. Defeating the Qin, Liu Bang declared himself the new emperor Gaozu. He believed that emperors should rule with a light hand, and not grind the people down with harsh decrees. When Gaozu died peacefully in 195 BCE, his heirs succeeded to the throne.

Trade and Learning

Under the Han emperors, Chang'an became a center of learning. The university there attracted scholars and poets from far and wide. The city lay at the heart of an efficient communications network set up by the Han rulers. A network of roads and canals connected the capital with distant parts of the empire.

Chang'an stood at the eastern end of the ancient trade route known as the Silk Road, which stretched nearly seven thousand miles (11,200 km) westward across central Asia as far as the Mediterranean and the Roman Empire.

Daily Life

Every morning the streets of Chang'an rang with the cries of city traders and beggars, the hammering of craftsmen, the music of street musicians, and other noises. Country people visiting to sell their crops at market marveled at the fine houses, temples, and graceful bridges. In the markets government officials watched to make sure that prices were fair and no one was cheated.

Later History of Chang'an

In 25 CE the peace at Chang'an was shattered by war and rebellion. The walls were breached, and much of the city was destroyed as the old Han regime was overthrown. The new rulers transferred the capital to Luoyang in the east. Five centuries later, a new dynasty, the Sui, united China after years of war and reinstated Chang'an as the capital. Under the next dynasty, the Tang (618–907), Chang'an became a great cultural center and probably the world's largest city, with over a million citizens.

SEE ALSO
- Cheng • China
- Roman Republic and Empire

Glossary

Akkadian An ancient Semitic language of Mesopotamia, used from around 2500 BCE.

anthropologist A scholar who studies the early history of a people.

artifact An ancient object made by humans; often one that comes to light through archaeological research.

bas-relief A type of sculpture in which the design projects slightly from a flat background.

city-state An independent state consisting of a city and its surrounding territory.

consul The leader of the Roman senate. A senior and junior consul were elected every year.

cuneiform A style of writing using wedge-shaped characters, usually made by a reed or other stylus pressed into a tablet of wet clay, which was then hardened in the sun or baked. The term also describes similar writing carved into material such as stone.

dowry The money or property brought by a woman to her marriage.

earthwork A structure, such as an embankment or a ditch, in which earth (soil) is the main building component.

Flood, the The great flood of the land mentioned in Mesopotamian mythology and the Old Testament of the Bible.

Hellenistic period The period of Greek civilization between the late fourth and first centuries BCE.

legion A Roman army division, consisting of between three and six thousand soldiers, or legionaries, including cavalry.

megalith A very large stone used in ancient times as a monument.

Neolithic Referring to a prehistoric period (the later Stone Age) marked by the establishment of settled villages, the development of farming, and the use of new types of artifacts such as polished stone, axes, and pottery. Neolithic culture appeared at different dates around the world, beginning around 7500 BCE in the Middle East.

obelisk A four-sided pillar that narrows towards the top.

Palaeolithic Referring to a time, also called the Old Stone Age, when people used primitive, chipped-stone tools.

papyrus A kind of reed that grows by rivers and in marshes in ancient Egypt. The stems of the reeds were beaten flat and laid over each other to make a smooth sheet that could be written upon and rolled up for storage.

pastoralism The keeping of domestic animals, like sheep and goats, for their milk and meat.

rhetoric The art of argument and persuasion, taught in ancient Greek and Roman schools.

scribe An official in ancient Egypt who could read and write.

Semitic Referring to languages related to modern Arabic and Hebrew.

senate The ruling legislative body of ancient Rome.

Seven Wonders of the World The seven structures that ancient scholars considered to be the most remarkable in the world. They comprise the pyramids of Egypt, the giant bronze statue of the god Apollo in Rhodes, the statue of Zeus at Olympia carved by Phidias, the temple of the goddess Artemis in Ephesus, the lighthouse of Alexandria, the mausoleum of Halicarnassus, and the Hanging Gardens of Babylon.

stylus A pointed instrument, usually a reed, used in ancient times for writing on clay.

Sumerian An early non-Semitic language of ancient Mesopotamia, used from around 3000 BCE.

sutra Buddha's teachings preserved in a written dialogue.

torc A large metal ring worn around the neck by the Celts. Torcs were made from metals such as bronze, silver, gold, and electrum (a mixture of silver and gold) and could be plain or decorated.

tribute Payment made by one state to another as a sign of submission.

ziggurat English word for *ziqquratu*, a temple built in the shape of a stepped pyramid, found in Mesopotamian cities.

zodiac An imaginary belt across the sky that holds twelve special constellations used to read horoscopes.

Index

Page numbers in **boldface type** refer to main articles.
Page numbers in *italic type* refer to illustrations.